INTRODUCING

Postfeminism

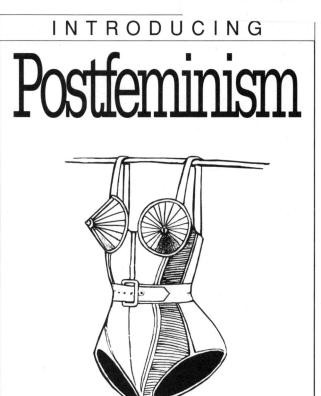

Sophia Phoca and Rebecca Wright

Edited by Richard Appignanesi

ICON BOOKS UK   TOTEM BOOKS USA

Published in the United Kingdom
in 1999 by Icon Books Ltd.,
Grange Road, Duxford,
Cambridge CB2 4QF
email: icon@mistral.co.uk
www.iconbooks.co.uk

Distributed in the UK, Europe,
Canada, South Africa and Asia by the
Penguin Group: Penguin Books Ltd.,
27 Wrights Lane, London W8 5TZ

Published in Australia in 1999
by Allen & Unwin Pty. Ltd.,
PO Box 8500, 9 Atchison Street,
St. Leonards NSW 2065

Published in the United States
in 1999 by Totem Books
Inquiries to: PO Box 223,
Canal Street Station,
New York, NY 10013

In the United States,
distributed to the trade by
National Book Network Inc.,
4720 Boston Way, Lanham,
Maryland 20706

Library of Congress Catalog
Card Number: 98–075005

What is Postfeminism?

Postfeminism does not mean feminism is over. It signifies a shift in feminist theory. Feminism is identified with a desire for gender equality in a long historic struggle which advocated change through political action. Feminism draws attention to the linguistic differentiation associated in English with the two adjectives for the terms woman and man. One adjectival derivation – **feminine** and **masculine** – is used by feminists to refer to social, cultural and psychic constructions. The other – **female** and **male** – represents the biological aspects of gendered identities. This linguistic distinction has been broadly understood as an ideological one which postfeminists have interrogated.

Postfeminism begins in *1968* . . .

. . . *three months before the revolutionary Events of May '68.*

Postfeminism has developed since the late 1960s from the deconstruction of patriarchal discourses. This is a development of feminism informed by the key analytical strategies of contemporary thought – psychoanalysis, poststructuralism, postmodernism and postcolonialism.

3

The Origins of Postfeminism

The first shift between feminism and postfeminism was marked by the following event: Paris, 8 March 1968 – International Women's Day. Members of the group *psychanalyse et politique* (later re-named *politique et psychanalyse,* or *po et psych*) marched through the city carrying placards reading "Down with Feminism".

French Feminisms

The *po et psych*, formed in 1968, was the cultural and intellectual centre for the MLF (*Mouvement de Libération des Femmes*). They established the publishing house, *des femmes*. The term MLF was coined by the French press in 1970 to identify the diverse feminist groups which had emerged in France since 1968. The two branches of the MLF – *féministes révolutionnaires* and the *po et psych* – became identified with two distinct forms of feminism. This distinction now characterizes the split between American and French feminism.

Antoinette Fouque (b. 1936), Member of the European Parliament (MEP), underwent psychoanalysis with Jacques Lacan between 1967 and 1974. In 1970, she was offered a Lectureship at Vincennes, University of Paris VIII. She was a co-founder of the MLF, spokesperson for the *po et psych* and creator of the publishing house *des femmes*.

*The movement had two orientations, one towards **equality**, the other towards **identity**. Identity in this context must be understood as the uniqueness of the other and not as sameness.*

Monique Wittig (b. 1935), Professor in the Department of French and Italian at the University of Arizona, spokesperson for the FR, started the journal *Questions Féministes* with Christine Delphy and Simone de Beauvoir. Wittig has disputed the biological origins of gender difference.

Woman is socially constructed, inscribed in the heterosexual binary framework of male and female. Lesbians therefore are not women because they are not dependent on a male definition of woman.

GABRIELLE D'ESTRÉES AND ONE OF HER SISTERS. 16TH CENTURY.

Women and lesbians are both cultural artefacts; but unlike women, lesbians refute the heterosexually-fixed connection between gender and sexuality.

féministes révolutionnaires

The group *féministes révolutionnaires* (FR) was established in 1970 as a faction of the MLF. They adopted what has become known as the American model of consciousness-raising groups and opposed Freudian psychoanalysis. The FR stood for equality and had separatist tendencies which were particularly supported by the lesbian members of the group.

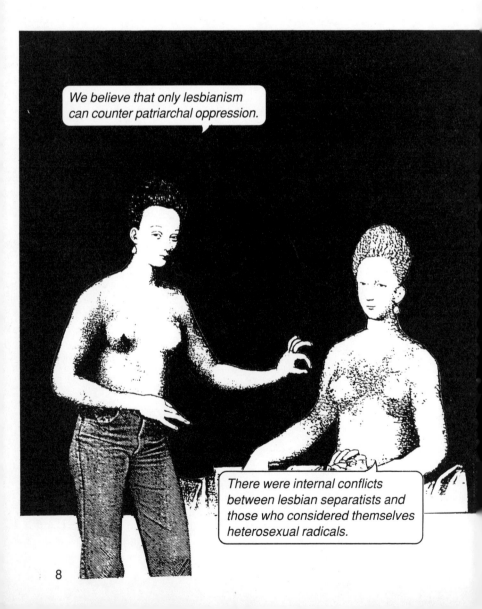

The FR opposed the *po et psych* group who preferred *difference* to what they saw as assimilation which will result from a desire for equality.

The FR sought visibility through the media and staged disruptive public actions. For example, a group of women (including Wittig) placed a wreath at the tomb of the Unknown Soldier in Paris.

To commemorate the unknown wife of the soldier.

We interrupted a Right to Life anti-abortion meeting and distributed bits of veal lung.

They staged *manifestations* on Mother's and Father's Days; organized "Days for Denouncing Crimes Against Women"; sit-ins to help unwed mothers; disruptions of government meetings.

Simone de Beauvoir (1908–86), influential writer and socialist, became a feminist in 1968 and a member of the FR. Beauvoir's classic **The Second Sex** (1949) is one of feminism's key texts. She has famously written: "One is not born, but rather becomes, a woman."

Women are socially constructed as feminine. In order to gain equality and emancipation, women should reject the socially oppressive constraints of femininity and adopt masculinity.

Although she regarded gender as a socially constructed category, she opposed the feminine on the grounds that femininity equals natural passivity and dependency in opposition to an active and independent masculinity.

The FR were powerful advocates against *biological determinism*: the idea that women are subordinate to the masculine norm.

*We reject psychoanalysis on the grounds that it is **biologically essentialist**.*

We prefer political processes which socially seek to reject patriarchy.

In the 1970s, this led to a re-valorization of female identity and motherhood, challenging the original notion that motherhood is a condition of oppression.

But what is essentialism?

Essentialism

Essentialism refers to the traditional notion that the identities of men and women are biologically, psychically and socially *fixed* or *determined*. The essentialist position therefore cannot acknowledge the possibility of any change.

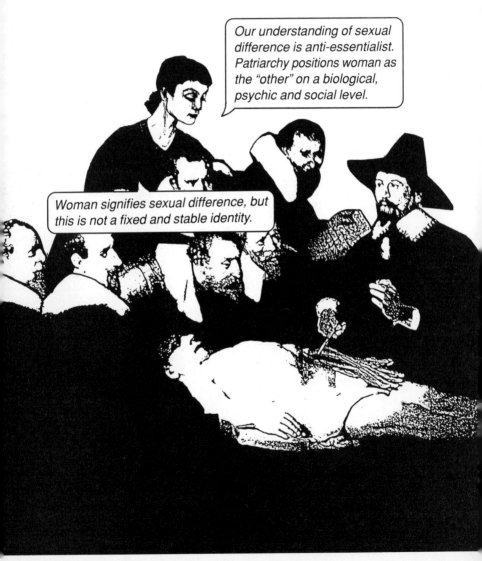

Essentialism is a very controversial term for feminism.

The Problem of Humanism

The classic European tradition of **humanism** upholds the view that human self-improvement and progress must be unlimited. Anti-humanists tend to emphasize the social, economic and psychological structures that *determine* and *limit* the ways in which individuals can act. Humanism can also, like essentialism, present a problem of fixed categories.

Humanism claims equality for **all** human beings. But this does not acknowledge that identity is constructed according to difference. For example, by claiming that men and women are equal, sexual difference becomes erased.

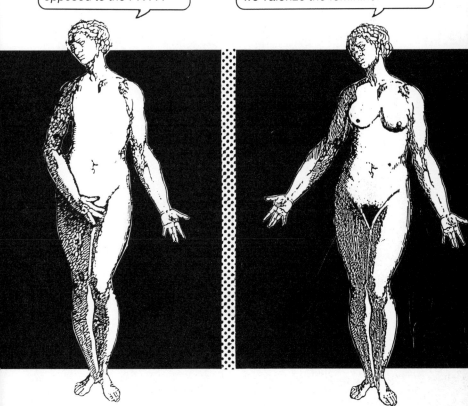

The *po et psych* faction emphasized difference as against assimilation which would be the end result of the FR's desire for equality.

The *po et psych*

The *po et psych* adopted psychoanalysis to explore women's libido and pleasure, women's fantasy and women's texts.

*We're looking at the relationship between **body** and **language**.*

*But the crucial use of psychoanalysis is to understand the operations of the **patriarchal unconscious**.*

These *po et psych* explorations in the mid-1970s drew on the theories of psychoanalysis and deconstruction established by Sigmund Freud, Jacques Lacan and Jacques Derrida, as we'll now see, beginning with Freud.

Freudian Psychoanalysis

"Psychoanalysis" was a term coined by its founder, **Sigmund Freud** (1856–1939). The key concept of psychoanalysis is that identity emerges in relation to sexuality and desire. Psychoanalysis refers to human beings as "subjects" to indicate that identity is subject to sexual desire and the **unconscious**.

The aim of psychoanalysis is to explain how unconscious processes are involved in constructing the subject.

Psychoanalysis is critically important to feminism because of its origin in Freud's challenge to an apparent female disorder, **hysteria**.

What is Hysteria?

The term "hysteria" comes from the Greek *hysteros*, meaning womb. Psychiatry in the late 19th century classified hysteria as an exclusively female pathological form of behaviour. It was originally characterized as a "uterine" disease and sometimes treated by direct medical attacks on the ovaries and the uterus itself. Freud reversed the established neurological diagnosis of hysteria in two ways.

The Case of Anna O.

In 1882, *Josef Breuer* (1842–1925), a friend and medical colleague of Freud, reported on a case of hysteria in a 21-year-old woman, "Anna O.". Her father had fallen seriously ill and she nursed him constantly until his death about a year later.

Her hallucinations in daytime became more violent after her father's death. But at night, she would mumble words in a state of trance. These trances led to Breuer's important discovery.

Breuer's Discovery: The Talking Cure

Breuer discovered that he could use Anna's trances to remove her symptoms by getting her to **talk** about "forgotten" memories. Anna named it her "talking cure". For instance, by this method of raising unpleasant memories, she recalled the first occasion when she began to squint. Once, while nursing her father, she had held back her tears so as not to upset him. But then he asked her the time . . .

And, as for the "hysterical" paralysis of the right arm and neck, this went back to a late night of exhaustion when she hallucinated and "saw" a black snake at her father's bedside . . .

Sexuality and the Unconscious

One unexpected side-effect of Breuer's "cathartic method" was that, as she improved, Anna O. fell in love with him and even announced that she was "pregnant with his child". This frightened Breuer and he fled. But it opened Freud's eyes to a possible deeper, **unconscious** sexual basis underlying the symptoms of neurotic illness.

*If only Breuer had treated Anna's "love" as another symptom, one more **disguise**, then he might have got to the bottom of the **sexual cause** of her disturbances . . .*

"Anna O." – her real name was **Bertha Pappenheim** (1856–1936) – eventually recovered and became a notable social worker and feminist.

The Story of Sexuality

Sexuality in psychoanalysis is not seen in the usual way as either "natural" or simply conditioned by biology. What we come to recognize as adult sexuality originates in infantile sexuality. Sexuality has a *pre-history*. It doesn't just suddenly "appear" in adulthood. For the first time, Freud recognized that there is a *narrative*, a "story to tell", in sexuality. This is the important thing to grasp.

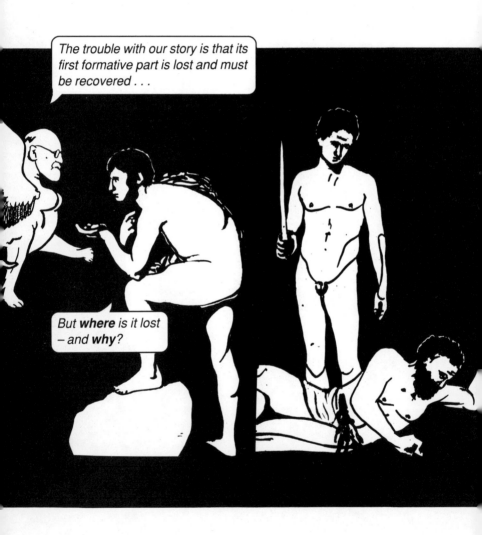

The trouble with our story is that its first formative part is lost and must be recovered . . .

*But **where** is it lost – and **why**?*

The Oedipus Complex

Freud places the crucial beginning of the story in childhood. A powerful desire for the mother, together with a murderous impulse against the father, emerges between the ages of three and five. This he called the **Oedipus Complex**, from the ancient Greek myth of Oedipus who unwittingly killed his father and married his mother. The tragedy of Oedipus, king of Thebes, was dramatized by *Sophocles* (c. 496–406 BC).

This early episode is forgotten – or repressed – but can later be responsible for unconscious guilt.

Freud allows for a "resolution" of the Oedipus Complex. But this is where the story becomes very problematical for feminists, and indeed all women, as we'll now see.

Difference and Penis Envy

"Difference" is another key word that we will often meet in this text. Now, for Freud, sexual difference is culturally established at the early stage of the Oedipus Complex. Its "resolution" makes the difference between male and female identities. The boy resolves his Oedipus Complex by renouncing a desire for the mother – because of the threat of castration that he imagines – and identifies with the patriarchal authority of the father.

She goes into the Oedipal phase desiring the mother, just like the boy, but then realizes that she lacks the "penis". She turns away from the mother – recognizing that she too is lacking – and develops a desire for the father.

I'll have a child from him that must fill the lack . . .

"Penis envy" characterizes the development of female sexuality. The girl's "anatomical lack" drives her to desire the paternal penis. To resolve the Oedipal Complex, she must then substitute this desire with the wish for a child.

So, the important "difference" we must conclude from Freud's story of sexual identity is that . . .

1. Masculinity and femininity are conditioned according to the **presence** and **absence** of the phallus.

2. There is only one kind of sexuality – and it is **phallic**.

3. In patriarchal terms, the phallus designates **superiority**.

4. The phallus and the Oedipus Complex are responsible for establishing the child's sexual identity and constructing the **unconscious**.

5. Freud has developed both male and female sexuality according to a single **masculine model**.

According to Freud, both genders go through the Oedipal stage.

They emerge desiring the opposite sex and identify with their same gender.

I object to the positioning of women as the inferior gender – a "second sex".

Simone de Beauvoir is right, but things aren't quite so bleak . . .

Is "penis envy" a biological fact or a psychical construct? Freud is ambiguous.

The ambiguity will allow later feminists, and especially postfeminists, to argue that gender is psychically constructed rather than pre-established biologically.

The Mother's Body

Melanie Klein (1882–1960), although not a feminist, developed a radical challenge to Freud's Oedipus Complex. But because she was seen as "essentialist" in her view of feminine drives, feminists have been slow to recognize her contributions.

Klein found that a girl experiences an equivalent to a boy's castration anxiety. She explained that the girl's fear was connected with the **mother's body**.

The girl fears that her hostility to her mother's insides (her ability to produce children) will cause her mother to retaliate and destroy the child's body.

This contradicted Freud's view at the time. He claimed that children deny the anatomical difference between mother and father.

Unlike Freud, Klein believed that girls have different fantasies to boys, and only women analysts can uncover them. She argued against Freud's notion that the Oedipus Complex starts with the genital phase (age three onwards), claiming that it begins earlier. She also suggested that the super-ego is not the outcome of the Oedipus Complex, but precedes it.

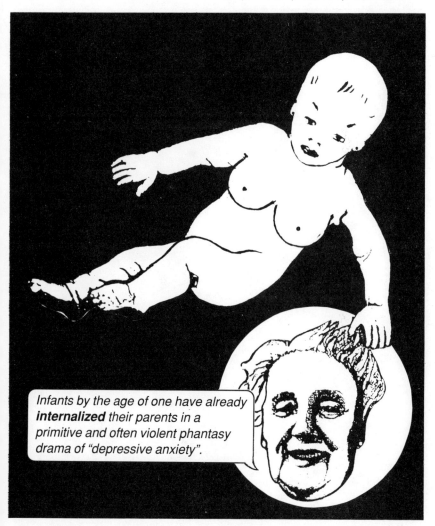

Infants by the age of one have already **internalized** their parents in a primitive and often violent phantasy drama of "depressive anxiety".

The infant must resolve the conflict "inside" itself of what is experienced either as **good** or **bad** objects in the earliest crucial phase of its development.

Object Relations

Klein pioneered the British "object-relations" school of psychoanalysis. She discovered that children use toys to display the drama of relations (to parents, family and others) that is taking place inside them.

Children's games with toys are connected to unconscious anxieties and inhibitions within them.

Klein encouraged the child to overcome its inhibitions by making interpretations between its games and its worries. The child's play was equivalent to the verbal technique of free association of ideas in the adult patient. A development from inhibited to more imaginative play gave clear evidence of successfully interpreting the child's deepest worries.

Conflict with Anna Freud

Anna Freud (1895–1982), Freud's daughter, was also working in this area of child analysis. She conflicted with Klein's view that all disturbances in children can be treated in a similar way to adult problems.

*My criticisms are based on a concern about being **too explicit** with children . . .*

Or is it based on a fear of probing the depths of the unconscious?

Klein put her faith in her radical discoveries about the child's inner world and its logic. She did not hesitate to treat even autistic children, and also went beyond Freud's limits of treating only neurotics, to pioneer analysis of psychotics, both adults and children.

The Womanly Masquerade

Joan Riviere (1883–1962), a colleague of Freud, was another non-feminist contributor to psychoanalysis. She was in analysis with both Freud and Klein, among others. In 1929 she published her famous paper, "Womanliness as masquerade", in the *International Journal of Psycho-Analysis*.

The paper refers to the case study of a successful professional woman who seeks reassurance from men by flirting.

She "performs" femininity so as to avert anxiety and the retribution feared from men.

Joan Riviere's essay has been regarded as a significant contribution to the development of the Oedipus Complex in women.

The primal Oedipal scene confronts Riviere's case study (and indeed other women) with her lack of the father's penis. She becomes phallic through her "masculine" success, but she attempts to conceal this by flirting and so taking up a "feminine" identity.

The reader may ask how I define womanliness or where I draw the line between genuine womanliness and the "masquerade". My suggestion is not, however, that there is any such difference; whether radical or superficial, they are the same thing.

For Riviere, femininity is constructed according to social codes through which the female subject becomes a woman by a process of mimesis. "Womanliness can be assumed and worn as a mask."

Linguistic Difference

Ferdinand de Saussure (1857–1913), a Swiss linguist, revolutionized our understanding of language. His linguistic theory provides access to the key intellectual movements that concern postfeminism. In his view, language is a system of signs. A sign is made up of a **signified** – a mental element (for example, the concept "dog") and a **signifier** – a physical element (the sound "dog" or its written symbol). The relationship between the two (Sr/Sd) is arbitrary and not one of correspondence. In other words . . .

The concept "dog" is denoted in English by the sound **d–o–g**.

Woman's best friend.

But in French the signifier sound is **chien**.

For Saussure, it is simply convention that links the signifier sound "dog" – or "chien" – to the signified concept.

The sound "dog" carries meaning only because it is different from the sound "dig".

Language works because of this underlying rule of **difference**. The "deep structures" of linguistic difference are independent of the human agents who use language. And it is this – the independence of the structure from its user – that established Saussure's revolution.

Structuralism

Saussure's theory displaces the human subject from the focus of investigative interest. What matters is the relationship that signs have to each other and their position within the system. Saussure breaks with the deeply-felt commonsense view that language somehow "means" reality. Language is instead structured to signify only itself. It is coherent, it has **use-value**, but does not correspond to reality. This structuralist model of language made its impact in the 1950s when the anthropologist *Claude Lévi-Strauss* (b. 1908) applied the binary opposition of signifier/signified to the study of "primitive" societies.

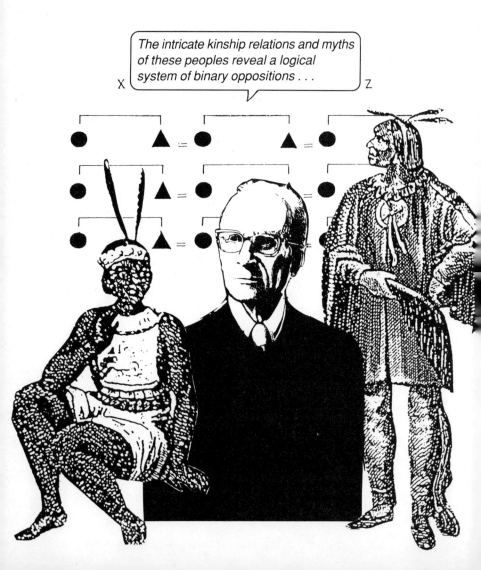

The intricate kinship relations and myths of these peoples reveal a logical system of binary oppositions . . .

Binary Oppositions

Lévi-Strauss believed he had solved the riddle of how culture is produced by the human mind. The shape of the social world is determined by the structure of the human mind, which everywhere and at all times thinks in **binary oppositions**. Structuralism was adopted by Barthes in literature, Foucault in history, Lacan in psychoanalysis – and many others. But in the late 1960s, their claims to a "solution" were severely criticized by Jacques Derrida and Barthes himself, who shifted over to "post-structuralism".

Saussure's notion of a "conventional" link between signifier and signified is very weak . . .

The pathways to meaning are a lot more complex and slippery.

*The relationship between signifier and signified is **motivated** rather than arbitrary. This is my view of post-structuralism.*

Post-structuralism was in fact a realization of the deeper radicalism lodged in the structuralist model of language. We are fast heading towards postmodernism! But before getting there, let's first consider the key ideas of Lacan in psychoanalysis.

A Linguistic Model of Psychoanalysis

The French psychoanalyst *Jacques Lacan* (1901–81) initiated a "back to Freud" movement. but with a radical difference that got him expelled from the orthodox ranks of Freudianism.

*I combined Freudian psychoanalysis with **semiotics** – the study of signs, codes and structures of language.*

He replaced Freud's psycho-dynamic model of **id**, **ego** and **super-ego** with a structuralist **linguistic** model – which helps to explain his famous declaration: "The unconscious is structured as a language."

The ID (Latin for "it") is the primitive, unconscious basis of the psyche dominated by primary urges.
The psyche of the newborn child is primarily id.
But contact with the external world modifies part of the id.
Perception of this difference is what modifies the EGO.

Ego development is imprinted by the instinctual structure of the libido (mouth, anus, genitals).

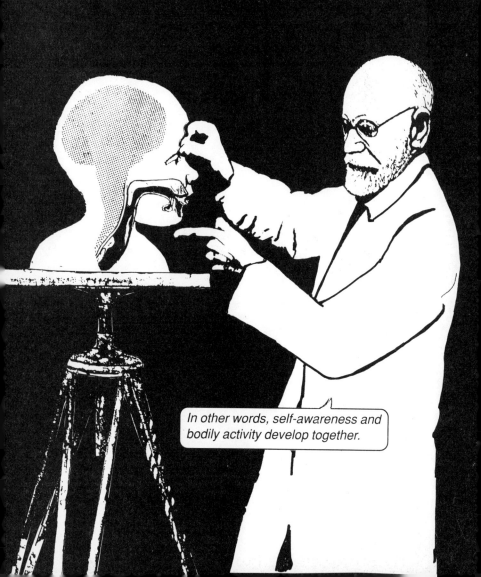

In other words, self-awareness and bodily activity develop together.

The Ego

Freud gives the ego several important functions.

The ego is a guide in reality. It can adapt or change.
Conscious perceptions belong to the ego. This is an aspect of the ego turned towards external reality.
But the ego also acts as an inhibiting agency.

*This other aspect of the ego is turned internally and functions **unconsciously**.*

For instance, the ego's repression of the id is unconscious. This is one of the ego's defence functions which are all unconscious.

The Super-Ego

The SUPER-EGO is not just a "conscience". It is the heir to the Oedipus Complex.

As the Oedipal impulses are repressed and disappear, their place is taken up by the super-ego.

The super-ego is introjected parental authority. It is the result of a defensive effort which prohibits the expression of Oedipal wishes.

Let's now examine the operations of Lacan's "Freudian linguistic" model.

The Imaginary and the Real

In the Imaginary order, the infant believes that s/he is part of the mother. The infant does not yet understand *difference*.

The child is born into the Real. This precedes the ego and the organization of the drives. The child does not perceive its subjectivity as a corporeal totality but as a fragmented set of sensory and perceptual experiences associated to plenitude and fullness.

The Real can only be conceptualized through the reconstruction of the Imaginary and the Symbolic orders. The Real is not the same as reality but is the "unassimilable", the "impossible".

The Mirror Phase: the Ego Ideal

Between six and eight months, the infant enters the **mirror stage**. The ego begins to be formed when the infant first recognizes its own image.

> The child perceives the reflection to be more complete than it imagined – an **ego ideal**.

Recognition is therefore overlaid with *mis*-recognition. For the first time, the child experiences *difference* between the self and the m/other. From this time on, the fullness the child has experienced so far is interrupted by lack. The mirror stage pre-dates language, but indicates that the child has lost the "pure plenitude" of the Real.

The Symbolic Order

The symbolic order is connected to the unconscious and to language. To the unconscious, first, in the way the father enters this order. He represents a split in the relationship between mother and child. The phallus stands for the "Law of the Father" and the fear of castration.

The child now begins to repress a desire for the imaginary unity with the maternal. The unconscious is linked to this repression and desire.

With the acquisition of language, the child recognizes difference. This difference indicates the separation from the mother. The speaking subject articulates identity – "I am" – through a recognition of difference and loss.

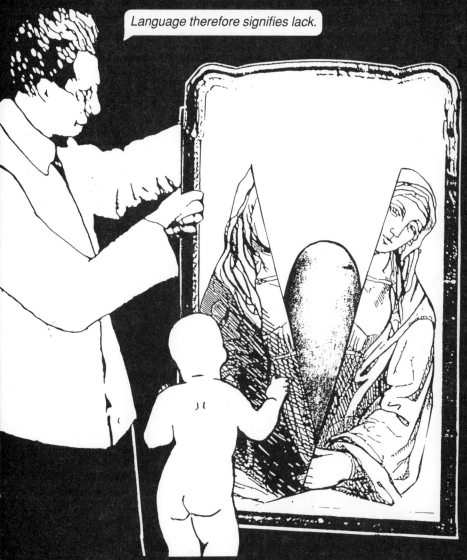

It is impossible to avoid the Symbolic because it would result in psychosis.

The Phallus and Feminist Criticism

In Lacan's model, the phallus is therefore a signifier of **lack** – not an actual organ.

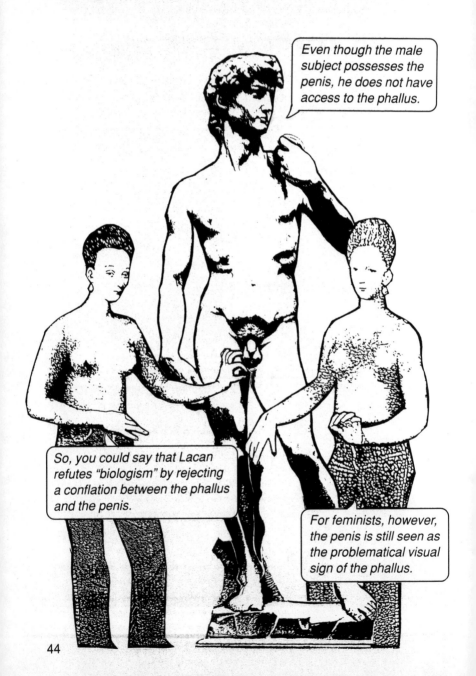

Even though the male subject possesses the penis, he does not have access to the phallus.

So, you could say that Lacan refutes "biologism" by rejecting a conflation between the phallus and the penis.

For feminists, however, the penis is still seen as the problematical visual sign of the phallus.

Some feminists have argued that Lacan's phallocentrism reveals how men and women are constructed according to patriarchal structures. In his model of psychoanalysis, Woman is nothing but an effect of phallic fantasy.

However, feminists have taken up the idea that because of her exclusion from the phallic economy, woman's relationship to the Real becomes more significant. Feminists have read Lacan in a variety of different ways which attempt to re-valorize the feminine.

Logocentrism and Deconstruction

Saussure's model of structural linguistics proposes that all meaning is constructed through binary oppositional differences. **Jacques Derrida** (b. 1930), the French philosopher, offers a post-structuralist deconstruction of this model.

?

male–female
presence–absence
spoken–written
white–black

But notice – one term always benefits over the other. Binary opposition **privileges** the first term – for instance, male over female.

What is "deconstruction"? It is not a method, because Derrida is against the trap of the systematic. Rather, it is a tactic to "protect" the "free play of the signifier". Deconstruction is designated as a double movement: both disordering, or disarranging, and also re-arranging.

What is "logocentrism"? Western thought has always looked for secure foundations: fundamentals, logical principles or a notion of the *centre*. These are the groundings for all its inquiries and statements.

The basic drive of Western thinking has been to ground truth in a single ultimate point – an ultimate origin.

This is what Derrida calls logocentrism. The *Logos* (from the Greek, "word", "reason", "reckoning") has bewitched us into the mistaken belief that meaning somehow exists "out there" and guarantees the truth of our statements.

Speech, Writing and *Différance*

Derrida draws our attention to one very important binarism – *writing* and *speech*. Speech is the privileged term, the one which (at least since Plato's time) has enshrined the origin of truth – *Logos* – "the Word made Flesh" as we find in St John's Gospel. What about writing, then?

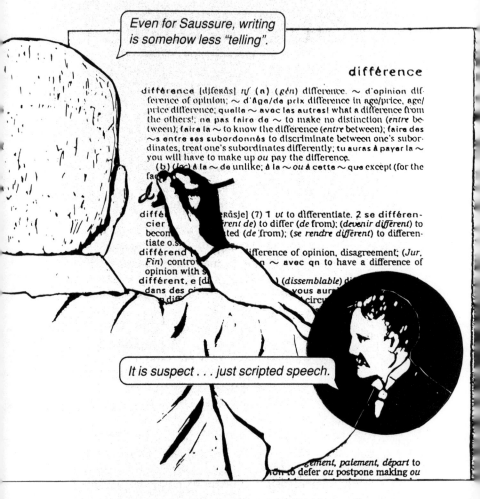

Even for Saussure, writing is somehow less "telling".

It is suspect . . . just scripted speech.

To combat this "repression of writing", Derrida coined the term *différance*. This is a play on the meanings of "difference" and "deferral", but it does not exist in any French dictionary. Its fiction cannot be detected by speaking it, but only when *written*. It is literally "unspeakable". This is one example of disrupting language (= meaning) by the "free play of the signifier".

Phallogocentrism

Postfeminism has gained from Derrida's strategies of linguistic disruption. His idea of an "unspeakable *différance*" could be seen as applying to the condition of repressed and unprivileged Woman. This is not a natural condition but a constructed one that can be exposed by a deconstructive criticism of "phallogocentrism". What does this term reveal?

Lacan emphasizes the privileged role of the **phallus** as a primary signifier in Western culture . . .

Add this to **logocentrism** and you will expose the fundamentalism of a phallogocentric culture.

Deconstruction has offered feminism new possibilities to expose and dislocate the foundational patriarchal binary oppositions – for instance, the privilege of male over female.

Writing: *écriture féminine*

Writing, with its "free play of the signifier", is open to the unrepressed recognition of woman's "unspeakable *différance*". *Écriture féminine* is an experimental writing of this type, motivated by a desire to "inscribe the feminine", which originated in France in the mid-1970s.

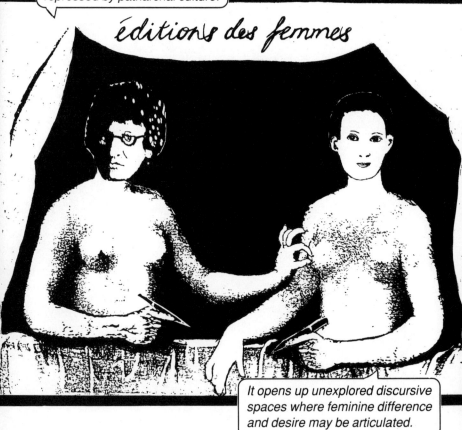

Écriture féminine *writes that for which there is no language – the feminine which has been repressed by patriarchal culture.*

It opens up unexplored discursive spaces where feminine difference and desire may be articulated.

Écriture féminine has been associated with the *po et psych* movement, the publisher *éditions des femmes* and the writer Hélène Cixous.

Hélène Cixous (b. 1937), Professor of English at Vincennes, University of Paris VIII, established the Centre d'Etudes Féminines in 1974.

Cixous supported the *po et psych* and *éditions des femmes*, but never became identified with a single movement or cause. She declared, "I am not a feminist."

Feminists want a place in the system, respect, social legitimation.

Cixous opposed these goals on the basis that they were identified with a bourgeois egalitarian demand for women to obtain power in patriarchal culture.

Sorties

Cixous seeks ways out – "*sorties*" – of structures which place woman in a binary system determined by her difference to man. For Cixous, Western philosophical discourse has constructed woman as a product of linguistic difference in binary oppositionality.

By destabilizing this binary structure, the privileging of the phallocentric subject will be undermined.

Cixous' writing is poetic, non-linear and anti-theoretical. She disrupts traditional frameworks and allows for contradictions. Cixous has valorized the hysteric in women's 20th century writing. Her concept of *écriture féminine* acknowledges Derrida's analysis of *différance*. Hélène Cixous was one of the earliest exponents of *écriture féminine* in her writing between 1975 and 1977.

The Imaginary

Cixous has established an understanding of the revolutionary potential of *écriture féminine*. Although she believes that *écriture féminine* is the province of both genders, she believes that women are closer to the feminine economy.

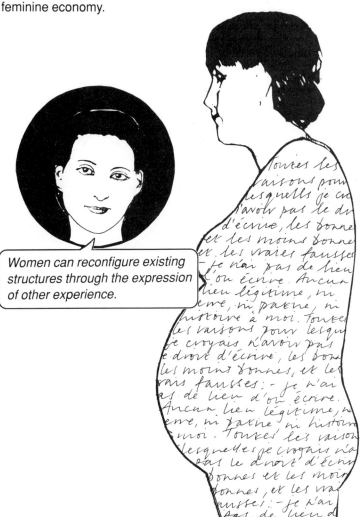

Women can reconfigure existing structures through the expression of other experience.

For Cixous, the inscription of the rhythms and articulation of the mother's body remains present in the adult. Cixous attaches special value to Lacan's Imaginary in the pre-symbolic union between the self and the m/other which becomes inscribed in language.

Feminine *Jouissance*

Cixous also sees another revolutionary potential in the feminine. The feminine acknowledges the other's difference and does not try to construct the self in the masculine position of dominance.

Feminine writing therefore allows for alternative dynamics of expression that do not rely on binary logic.

She produces texts which "write her body" and therefore destroy the closure of binary opposites. The pleasure of this open-ended textuality is referred to as *jouissance*. Coined by Lacan, this French term has no equivalent in English. It connotes the extreme pleasure derived from sexual orgasm.

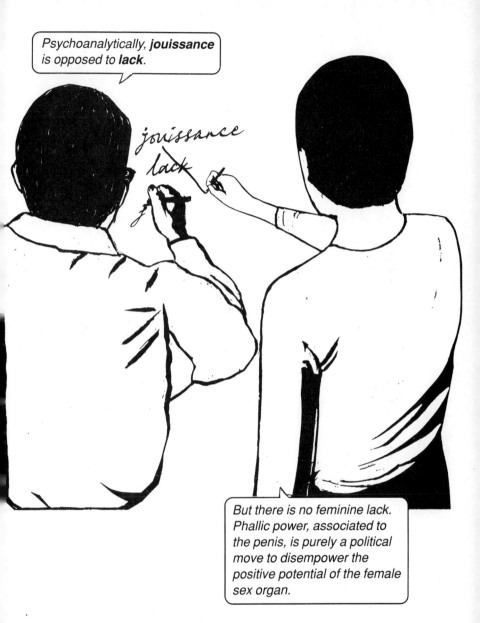

Textual *jouissance* is like the female erotic which cannot be theorized, enclosed or coded. Cixous' idea of **bisexuality** is closely related to Derrida's view of writing. For Cixous, writing is bisexual, although once again writing is more the province of women than of men.

Another key figure of French postfeminism is **Luce Irigaray** (b. 1932), a psychoanalyst specializing in psycho-linguistics. Since 1964 she has held a research post at the Centre National des Recherches Scientifiques. Irigaray was famously expelled from Lacan's École Freudienne at Vincennes after publishing *Speculum de L'Autre Femme*, 1974.

The École Freudienne considered me too political.

Irigaray's work celebrates femininity by offering a psychoanalytic critique of patriarchy. Her writing is poetic and philosophical. Like Cixous, Irigaray employs *écriture féminine* and advocates "writing the body".

Psychoanalysis is not sufficiently aware of the fact that its discourses, like others, are historically and culturally determined.

Psychoanalysis has not been able to access and therefore analyze its own unconscious fantasies.

Psychoanalysis is patriarchal, phallocentric and has not sufficiently recognized the role of the maternal or female sexuality.

Irigaray is critical of the ways in which psychoanalysis is transmitted from "father" to "son" – always in a *male* lineage – where identification with the father and devotion to his law are privileged.

Irigaray's Critique of Lacanian Psychoanalysis

Irigaray was informed by Lacan's reading of Freud and the Lacanian emphasis on the role of language in determining the formation of the unconscious. She attended Lacan's seminars, and he was her mentor.

For Lacan, the phallus is the privileged signifier marking the articulation of language and desire. He privileges the body as *male* in the mirror stage. The female body is reduced to a "hole".

To see what is specific to women, he would need a mirror which can look inside – the **speculum**.

?

Irigaray stresses a female reading of culture which deconstructs patriarchy and seeks alternatives in a utopian post-patriarchal future. She has employed Derridian deconstruction to trace "the masculine imaginary" in major philosophical texts and "interrogate the philosophical tradition, particularly from the feminine side".

Irigaray attempts to reveal what metaphysical constructions tend to conceal – the unacknowledged mother.

All Western culture rests on the murder of the mother.

Women do not exist in patriarchal representation.

This absence remains unrecognized because women's difference is not symbolized.

Irigaray conceptualizes a future where sexual difference is recognized by giving the maternal equal status to the paternal. To do this, women should return to a pre-Oedipal imaginary, a pre-patriarchal space before language.

Irigaray has been criticized for proposing an essentialist understanding of female sexuality which assumes a connection between the body and the "true self".

Kristeva and Feminism

Julia Kristeva (b. 1941), born in Bulgaria, came to France in 1965 with a formation in Russian semiotics and Marxism. She is Professor at the University of Paris VII, a semiotician, linguist and practising psychoanalyst. She combines linguistic theory with psychoanalysis. Her writing concentrates on the speaking subject.

I refuse to call myself a feminist. I refute the feminist use of the term "woman".

Kristeva's critiques reflect the reformist view of feminism put forward by the *po et psych*. She opposes a "feminism" – which she often refers to in inverted commas – because it has sought power in existing frameworks. Feminism in English-speaking countries, or what is known as Anglo-American feminism, she calls "bourgeois" and "liberal", and therefore not representative of the politics which are now broadly associated with the

Nevertheless, Kristeva has continued to oppose patriarchal power. She has described the feminist movement as a "movement of hysterics". Hysteria is not an undermining term in her view of psychoanalysis.

The feminist becomes "hysteric" because she is taken up by a patriarchal discourse which equates femininity with **lack**.

Kristeva's anti-feminist position stems from a concern that it will be co-opted by master discourses. Although Kristeva sees femininity as other to meaning and language, it must exist within the symbolic and the Law.

Kristeva's Semiotic

Kristeva has reconceptualized Lacan's distinction between the imaginary and the symbolic in her own terms of the *semiotic* and the symbolic. She has ventured far beyond Saussure's idea of the semiotic as simply the formal study of signs and significations. For her, the semiotic is linked to the pre-Oedipal primary impulses, the infant's earliest libidinal drives in deep relation to the maternal. The unpredictable and disruptive power of utterance, especially in poetry, can be traced back to this first stage in the formation of subjectivity.

The symbolic is instead connected to the formation of identity in the patriarchal order of social and signifying law.

*But it is the maternally defined semiotic which acts as a disruptive and **creative** force on the patriarchal symbolic.*

The Chora

The tension between the patriarchal symbolic order of law and the semiotic can be exemplified like this. Patriarchy operates on the binary logic of exclusion – a strict choice between One or the Other (A or non-A), but not both. The semiotic (or poetic) utterance accepts the contradiction that One and the Other exist simultaneously. Kristeva explains the "uncanniness" of the semiotic by reference to the Greek term *chora* from **Plato** (427–347 BC) in his *Timaeus*. There, it means an unnameable, chaotic "womb-like" space existing prior to nameable Form. For Kristeva, the chora is the shared body space of mother and child which resists representation, but remains experienced as desire.

The chora is the **unspeakable** which leaves its presignifying traces in the "musicality" and kinetic rhythms of language.

The maternal chora precedes and underlies the possibility of signification – and also threatens to destabilize its order.

The Thetic and the Symbolic

Kristeva borrows another term, *thetic* ("positing"), from the German philosopher **J.G. Fichte** (1762–1814), meaning a judgement that affirms self-identity. Kristeva uses the thetic to mean the pre-symbolic stage at which the semiotic becomes temporarily ordered to allow for the transition to the symbolic. Kristeva follows the Lacanian model of the mirror phase.

This is the moment when the child's separation from the mother is achieved by a sense of threatened castration.

The resolution of the Oedipus Complex means that the child establishes his or her identity in relation to the phallus.

Upon entering the symbolic order, the subject represses the chora, and it can only be perceived as "pulsational pressure" within the order of symbolic language.

These "pressures" are signified as ruptures in language – the slippages, gaps or contradictions in meaning.

What is meant by "slippages" in language can be seen in the difference between scientific and poetic language. Science represses the semiotic and permits little or no slippage between description and thing. Poetry instead welcomes the semiotic ruptures of syntax, musical rhythms, the transgressions of sense through metaphor and other word play. Such evidence of disruption challenges any closure of linguistic theory, and yet, for Kristeva, semiotic theory is paradoxically both subversive and dependent on the law.

Bodily Horror and Abjection

The uncanny irruptions of the semiotic in conflict with the symbolic law can also be recognized in the language of bodily prohibitions or taboos. In the *Powers of Horror* (1980), Kristeva applies *sémanalyse* – her blend of semiotics and analysis – to the Biblical themes of defilement, abomination and sin. She also focuses on the French writer **Louis-Ferdinand Céline** (1894–1961), a virulent anti-Semite, pro-Nazi and wartime collaborator. Céline writes in rhythmic slang which aims to break all taboos by extreme scandalous abjection. He confesses to a relationship with his mother, a lace-maker, that has made him an unmasculine expert in every variety of lace.

But it has given him another insight, as he says in **Death on the Instalment Plan** . . .

. . . those females can wreck the infinite!

Céline expresses a fear of the chora – the maternal body as infinite space and maternal desire that threaten to wreck the lawful identity of patriarchal man. "Abjection", as defined by Kristeva, is manifest in cultural taboos. The abject taboo – for instance, bodily fluids – marks the sites which develop into the erotogenic zones – eyes, mouth, nose, anus, genitals. These zones are associated with the ingestion and expulsion of unclean, defiled or prohibited objects. The abject therefore emerges at the symbolic boundary between the inside and outside of the body. The Oedipalized subject attempts to expel unlawful objects by an elaborate construction of taboos.

French Versus Anglo-American Feminism

British and American feminism has been characterized by its aim of undermining patriarchy through changing the **social structures** in family and labour relations.

French postfeminism desires instead to establish a place for women in **discourse**, and that way to undermine patriarchal power.

Although this distinction is useful, it should be taken into account that some British feminists, especially Juliet Mitchell, defended Freud and Lacan, and that American feminists have been influenced by the work of Cixous, Irigaray and Kristeva who have challenged the dominance of the Lacanian "symbolic law".

Challenges within Anti-Essentialism

In the early 1970s, British feminists criticized essentialism from a Marxist perspective. Essentialism was seen to support the ideological notion that human nature is innate and therefore cannot be changed.

Sexual difference is socially and historically constructed, rather than biologically.

So-called "natural" categories of gender and sexuality require a Marxist materialist explanation.

But in the early 1980s, Lacanian psychoanalysis became endorsed because it too supported a non-essentialist standpoint.

Lacan theorized femininity as a non-biological category which allowed for the feminine position to be taken up by both genders. Lacanian anti-essentialism differed from the earlier materialist version in that it did not offer a promise of change which relied on a historical or social framework. Critics of Lacanian feminism have argued that his account of femininity continues to rely on biology because the penis "stands" in for the phallus. The Lacanian symbolic relies on this construction.

Juliet Mitchell (b. 1940), in her pioneering book **Psychoanalysis and Feminism** (1974), marked a shift in Anglo-American feminist theory. She argued that Freud's theories had been misunderstood and misinterpreted by feminists. Freud's theories were not motivated by a desire to advocate male dominance but, through observation, he revealed how patriarchal culture positions women. Freud is descriptive and not prescriptive. Psychoanalysis therefore offers feminists an insight into how patriarchal ideology is internalized by both men and women. And it also offers feminism an understanding, not otherwise possible, of sexual difference which does not rely on biology.

*Freudian analysis shows how gender roles are a consequence of **power** relations.*

Mitchell rejects both **naturalism**, which assumes a biological evolution of identity, and the **environmentalist** view which explains identity as a product of behavioural conditioning. Identity is therefore either "naturally" given or "environmentally" produced.

Psychoanalysis is a way of politicizing sexual difference. It offers an explanatory model rather than a therapeutic technique.

Decoding Popular Culture

Roland Barthes (1915–80) was Professor of Semiology at the Collège de France from 1976. His criticism of the "visual texts" of popular culture in **Mythologies** (1957) draws on Saussure's linguistic model of semiology and a Marxist theory of ideology. Barthes shows how the denotation of an image (e.g. the dots and colours of a photograph) constitutes the **signifier** and how the concept (e.g. of the young black man saluting the French flag) makes up the **signified**.

This new signifier conceals a hidden signified – *a connoted meaning* – that France is a great Empire.

Racism, sexism and colonialism are masked by the "natural appearance" of culture, and this is what Barthes means by "myths".

"Myths" serve to subsume difference under the familiar and the universal. For Barthes, all cultural products should be available for ideological and semiological criticism. His methods have been used extensively by feminist cultural theorists to analyze the sexist connotations of popular culture . . .

. . . Especially in advertising.

Barthes also empowered a critical reading of cultural artefacts in the way he demythologized texts. In his 1968 essay, "The Death of the Author", Barthes famously denied that the author alone determines the meaning of a text or has sole privileged access to it. Texts are the results of "a thousand sources of culture". The author is dead. But the *reader* is reborn as the creator of meanings.

Advertising the Body

Advertising is focused on controlling and preserving the contemporary subject, regardless of gender. The vast range of dietary, slimming, exercise, cosmetic and body maintenance products are advertised as a means of "preserving" the body. Consumer culture markets the concept of *self-preservation* by offering products which will combat physical deterioration and decay.

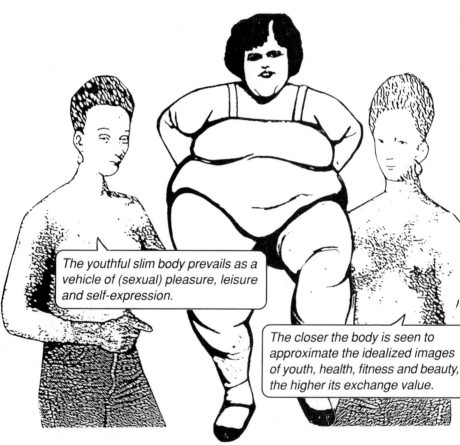

The youthful slim body prevails as a vehicle of (sexual) pleasure, leisure and self-expression.

The closer the body is seen to approximate the idealized images of youth, health, fitness and beauty, the higher its exchange value.

Advertising demands that individuals assume responsibility for the way they look by slimming, exercising or even cosmetic surgery. Wrinkles, fat, sagging flesh, loss of hair are all seen as signs of "moral decay", or in Kristeva's terms, "abjection".

This proliferation of images in consumer culture is increasingly addressed to both genders.

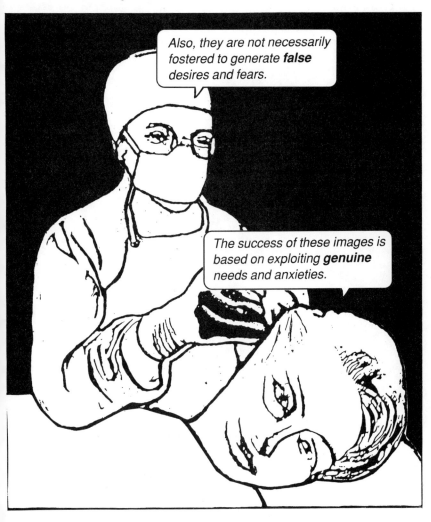

The desire for youth, beauty, health and sexual fulfilment are genuine preoccupations and longings. As a result of this flood of idealized hyperreal images, the difference between the authentic and the artificial body is being eroded. The contemporary subject is invited to construct a "post-human" subjectivity which flaunts fakery – for example, through cosmetic surgery.

The Body and the Gaze

In art and popular culture, the female body has functioned as spectacle. Woman offers her body to be surveyed. As the British art critic John Berger put it, back in the 1960s: "Men look at women. Women watch themselves being looked at."

She is often found surveying herself in the mirror, bathing or naked among a group of dressed men.

. . . presented as the object of the male gaze.

In the mid-1980s, erotic images of men began to appear in advertising. These images (e.g. in Levi jeans ads) were drawn from gay eroticism. For men to put their bodies on display contradicts previous codes of who *looks* and who is *looked at*. Feminism and gay activism have had a significant impact in challenging the traditional codes of the gaze.

Susan Sontag (b. 1933) is an American cultural critic and fiction writer. She has published essays on a vast range of subjects: philosophy, style, "camp", film, pornography, fascism, photography, and illness. But the main issues she tackles are concerned with aesthetics and ethics.

Her critical essay on **Illness as Metaphor** (1978) examines how illnesses such as TB and cancer have been seen as mysterious afflictions.

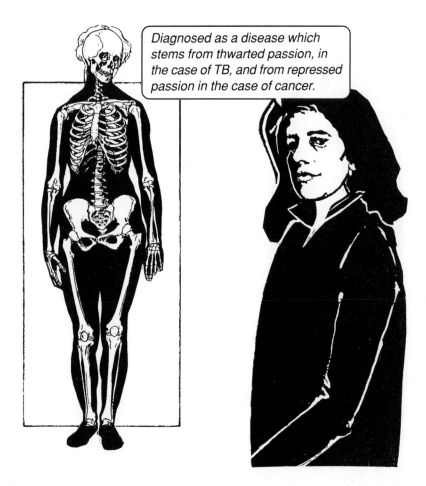

Diagnosed as a disease which stems from thwarted passion, in the case of TB, and from repressed passion in the case of cancer.

Metaphors are constructed according to the trends of the times.

In another essay, **AIDS and its Metaphors** (1989), Sontag looks at how the media's response to AIDS has been inscribed with metaphors of dread, with disastrous consequences. The accusatory aspect of these "metaphors of empowerment" propose that willpower can be summoned by the sick to resist illness.

*In the decade since I wrote **Illness as Metaphor** - and was cured of my own cancer, confounding my doctor's pessimism - attitudes about cancer have evolved...the word cancer is uttered more freely, and people are not often described anymore in obituaries as dying of a "very long illness".*

If illnesses continue to be seen as a plague, a curse, a social or a psychosomatic problem, the ill must remain isolated.

Camille Paglia (b. 1947), Professor of Humanities at the University of the Arts in Philadelphia, is a controversial figure in cultural theory who has pursued high-profile publicity.

> *If civilization had been left in female hands, we would still be living in female huts.*

Paglia writes in soundbites and draws on a wide range of literary and popular references. She proclaims a disaffection with the second wave of feminism, which she criticizes as "victim feminism". She is renowned for her controversial theories on date rape, suggesting that women should take the responsibility to avoid such situations.

Paglia promotes the pop icon Madonna as a role model for "true feminism".

She has taught young women to be fully female and sexual, while still exercising control over their lives.

Paglia has an essentialist understanding of gender, with sexual difference rooted in biology. Masculinity and femininity are constructed according to a binary model: masculine signifies active, and feminine equals passive. She combines this essentialism with a libertine notion of sexuality. We shall encounter other feminist "libertines" in our examination of pornography.

Romantic Fiction and Pornography

Feminists have objected to the representations of women in the fictions of "romantic love" and pornography. Both reaffirm the subordinate position of women within patriarchal culture.

In romantic fiction – a so-called women's genre – women arouse desire through virginal goodness which must result in marriage.

In pornography, women are reduced to passive, desiring bodies, always available for servicing men sexually.

Feminists Against Pornography

Pornography has been an extremely divisive issue for feminism. Feminists identified with the anti-pornography campaigners demand that women should change their fantasies if the content is oppressive to women. A moral charge is made that sexuality dehumanizes. This view corresponds to the charges made by right-wing crusaders. Explicit representations of sexuality corrupt the Christian view that sexuality should take place heterosexually within marriage. Sex should not be associated with passion which is seen to be potentially disruptive.

Andrea Dworkin (b. 1946) is one of the key anti-porn campaigners.

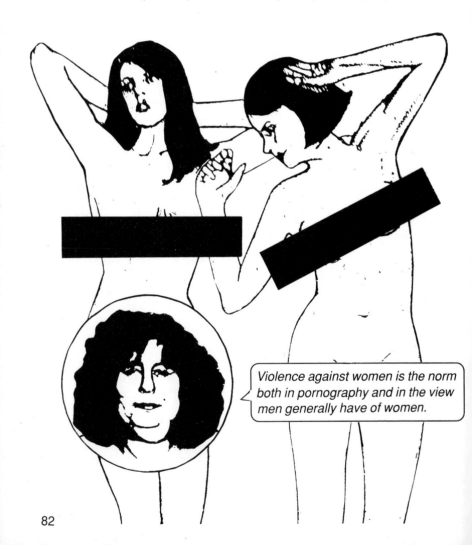

Violence against women is the norm both in pornography and in the view men generally have of women.

Feminists Against Censorship

Other feminists accept that fantasy is intrinsic to human beings and cannot be policed. Calls for censorship cut short women's exploration of their own sexuality and ways to express it. In psychoanalysis, desire arises in relation to a *wished-for* satisfaction, not an object.

Libertine Feminists

The notorious libertine **Marquis de Sade** (1740–1814) created an extreme fictional world in which sexual power-dynamics acted as a metaphor for social relations. His writings have influenced many intellectuals and writers who believe in transgressing and subverting the conservative "moral majority". Feminist "libertines" – for example, **Susan Sontag** and British novelist **Angela Carter** (1947–92) – are against "soft core" pornography or "erotica".

Soft core is ineffectually mundane and informed by the hedonism of consumer culture.

Libertines defend S&M or "hard core" pornography as a transgressive experience which achieves avantgarde subversion and excess.

Lesbians have claimed S&M, previously seen as the privileged space of the powerful, to transform the suffering experienced as a result of social powerlessness into pleasure.

Postmodernism and Postfeminism

"Postmodernism" maps out the contemporary experience of seismic crises in the foundations of Western modernity. New technologies in this age of "late" capitalism have transformed our spatial and temporal view of the planet and reconceptualized identity and history.

This is what we shall now explore by looking at some major "geographers" of postmodernism. Jacques Derrida, as we have already seen, is a key figure in postmodern philosophy. But the first crucial diagnosis of postmodernism as such came from *Jean-François Lyotard* (1924–98), Professor at the University of Paris VIII, in his book **The Postmodern Condition** (1979).

What is Postmodernism?

For Lyotard, postmodernism is characterized by the crisis in the legitimation of knowledge in the post-industrial age. The postmodern condition for him means the collapse of the grand- or meta-narratives which have legitimated the truth of history. His analysis is focused on **epistemology** (theories of knowledge) and **science**.

Lyotard traces two versions of narrative legitimation.

1. The **political** narrative which since the 18th century Enlightenment has promised progressive emancipation and freedom.

2. The **scientific** narrative which offers a "means to an end".

What Makes Science Legitimate?

The scientific narrative is legitimated because it ultimately offers the subject the promise of freedom. Scientific knowledge therefore does not find legitimation in itself but in the grand narratives of justice, humanity and emancipation. From a philosophical perspective, scientific knowledge does not rely on the principles of justice and legitimation, but on what Lyotard has termed the "metaprinciple of speculation".

Knowledge as Techno-Consumerism

In the age of postmodernism, scientific legitimation based on discourses of emancipation or speculation has lost credibility. This is partly due to "technoscience" – the impact of digital technologies on the control of information in late capitalism. For Lyotard, postmodern *de*-legitimation is inherent in the history of the legitimation of knowledge. He asks: "What proof is there that my proof is true?" Knowledge legitimates itself by citing its own operations as truth. But scientific knowledge cannot guarantee or control *other* discourses.

*Digital information-processing brings knowledge into **consumerism** and allows more local freedom.*

A variety of discourses and "micro"- narratives have emerged which cannot be encompassed in a notion of a single universal "meta"-narrative. The collapse of the grand-narratives allows a complexity of other local "small stories".

Feminism and Postmodernism

Initially, debates within postmodernism had little to do with feminism, and nor did feminism with postmodernism. More recently, however, postmodernism has offered feminism ways in which to conceptualize its own ongoing dilemma: the desire to seek equality within the very institutions and discourses which feminists have attempted to challenge and dismantle.

Central to Lyotard's idea of postmodernism is the notion that emancipatory discourses are no longer possible because there is no longer a belief in the truth of **foundational** meta-discourses (a slightly different "take" on Derrida's position).

The postmodern crisis in legitimation has meant that feminists also had to develop a self-reflexive questioning of their own legitimating procedures.

Feminism, like psychoanalysis, stems from **modernity**. Modern concepts of truth, justice and subjectivity emerged in the Enlightenment with the belief that human beings are committed to progress in moral and intellectual self-realization through reason.

A Theory of Hyperreality

Jean Baudrillard (b. 1929) taught sociology from 1966 to 1987 at the University of Nanterre. He achieved notoriety by claiming that postmodernity is an "age of simulation". By this he means that signs no longer reflect any reality whatsoever but are entirely self-referential, or **simulacra**. "Reality is over", it is erased, and what we have is residual nostalgia and **hyperreality**. Disneyland is the perfect example of the "simulacral world" which is more real than the memory of the real.

Disneyland disguises the fact that America is itself constituted by simulations.

Baudrillard published three articles on the Gulf War in the Paris newspaper, *Libération* (1991). For him, the war never actually "happened". This was a virtual war of information, electronics and images – not primarily of force. The more we have access to "live" war events, the more the reality becomes "media-massaged" information – which affected the way the event was actually conducted.

Most of the journalists at the front got their information from CNN on satellite TV.

The "enemy" was not challenged or annihilated. Iraqi dictator Saddam Hussein was left in place to ensure that US interests were left uncompromised. The subsequent peace was as much a simulation as the war.

Pastiche and Parody

Fredric Jameson (b. 1934), Professor of Literature at Duke University, argues that modernist "style" was established on avantgarde notions of originality and shock. These have now been replaced by what he refers to as "irrational eclecticism", in particular by pastiche as a postmodern form of parody. There is an important distinction between the two.

Parody redeploys meaning by imitating the myth of originality through repetition.

Pastiche instead acts as a nostalgic form of borrowing. It is mimicry which homogenizes everything in an indiscriminate and seemingly value-free way.

Parody can become politically invested, as it was in the modernist avantgardes of Dadaism, Surrealism and so on.

Cultural representation in postmodernity no longer refers to the real, but instead reduces the real to **spectacle**. Nostalgia films reproduce history as an "aesthetic effect" without a referent. For Jameson, this is an occasion for mourning because it undermines the Marxist legitimation of the socially progressive class struggle.

The Genealogy of Power

Michel Foucault (1926–84) was Professor of History and Systems of Thought at the Collège de France. Foucault's "archaeology" of modern society, as it emerged from the 18th century, reveals a **disciplinary** society which employs regulation rather than force to control its subjects. It functions by dividing or fragmenting its subjects into regulatory categories of place, function and attribution. Contemporary subjects are straitjacketed into binaries . . .

Mad/sane . . . sick/healthy . . . abnormal/normal

> This system works because people "subject" themselves to its norms and so regulate **themselves** in relation to society.

Foucault traces a "genealogy" (a history which supports current political practice) which has given rise to this self-legitimating system of regulation and control.

Foucault locates two historical events of particular "genealogical" significance to this regulatory system. The first is the reorganization of the city as a result of the plague at the end of the 17th century.

Subjects were categorized and regulated according to their sick or healthy status.

A system of power was introduced in which individuals were required to comply with a set of surveillance techniques contrived to assess people according to their moral and physical health.

The rise of a modern prison system, allied to the disciplinary surveillance of health, was exemplified by the **panopticon**, as we'll now see.

The Panopticon

The panopticon was a model prison designed by the Utilitarian philosopher *Jeremy Bentham* (1748–1832). The cells are arranged in a circle so that each one can be scrutinized from a central watchtower, the effect of this being that the prisoners feel continually watched, whether they actually are or not.

They begin to survey themselves, so that the exercise of discipline is no longer necessary.

The panopticon is a mechanism of power reduced to its ideal form. This system of surveillance is, for Foucault, applicable to all institutional systems of power. Power relations should therefore be analyzed at all levels, not necessarily in large-scale social "macro-"structures but on the local individual "micro-"level.

On Positive Sexuality: *Scientia Sexualis*

Discourses on sex which emerged in the 19th century medico-psychiatric milieu show that techniques of power which regulate the individual will work most effectively when concealed and seemingly **positive**. Power does not operate through the repression of sex, but through increasingly "open" discussion and analysis of it which promote notions of "abnormal" or "normal" sexuality. A scientific discourse of sex was produced in the 19th century, which Foucault termed *scientia sexualis*. At stake was not sex but the dynamics of power inherent in the scientific discourse itself.

Scientia sexualis *became another means of cataloguing and regulating the human subject which ends by entering the "liberationist" discourse of a healthy, positive sex-life.*

Confession is Good For You

Foucault cites **confession** as an effective and positive means of controlling the sexual subject. Originally a Christian rite of penance, the confession became a medical discourse of truth. We can see the "medicalized" confession everywhere now in different forms – in questionnaires along the lines of the Kinsey Report (1948–53), on the shrink's couch and on TV chat shows. Although subjects may reveal their most hidden pleasures, the understanding and cataloguing of these pleasures is inadequate.

*A scientific system has to be established which both **produces** and **governs** the sexual subject according to its norms.*

Scientia sexualis not only demands that the subject confesses, but also reveals the truth about the self to the self. As a result, liberationist groups have misunderstood *scientia sexualis* as a strategy for freedom, rather than as an effect of power.

Feminist Critiques of Foucault

Although Foucault has developed an important account of power, he does not focus on how individuals actually experience and exercise power. For him, individuals "are always in the position of simultaneously undergoing and exercising power". Power is not simply an effect of the state's domination of the individual – or a result of one group or individual oppressing another. The state's power to produce a totalizing web of control is dependent on its ability to co-opt the individual's **participation**.

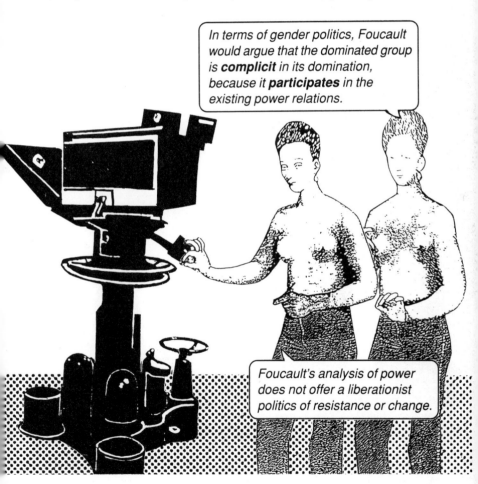

*In terms of gender politics, Foucault would argue that the dominated group is **complicit** in its domination, because it **participates** in the existing power relations.*

Foucault's analysis of power does not offer a liberationist politics of resistance or change.

Let's now turn to some of the key postfeminists who have criticized, but also been influenced by, postmodern theories.

Gynesis

Alice Jardine (b. 1951) is Associate Professor of Romance Languages and Literature at Harvard University. She draws on the writings of various French theorists, such as Lacan and Derrida. Jardine looks at how their work is marked by **gynesis** – a play on the word *gen*-esis/*gyn*-esis.

Jardine has coined the term gynesis in critical reference to the master or "grand" narratives that Lyotard and other postmodernists believe have collapsed. Gynesis is for her a space coded as "feminine".

This space has eluded the master narratives whose key topics of philosophy are established on notions of Man, Truth and History.

Although theorists like Derrida have used terms like "hymen" and "invaginated text" to challenge phallogocentric discourse, they do not relate this process of gynesis to women or feminism.

Psychoanalysis and Lesbianism

Jardine believes that postmodernism is more indebted to feminism than has been acknowledged. This is perhaps because feminism's contribution to postmodernism has been in the sensitive area of female sexuality, and indeed, homosexuality. Let's trace the "genealogy" back to Freud.

Freud attributed female homosexuality to the woman's "masculinity complex". He did not locate women's homosexuality in the specific "psychic economy" of femininity. Male and female homosexuality are not specified as *different*. This is Freud's explanation of "repressed homosexuality" in the famous case of Dora. Dora is said to harbour an "unconscious revenge fantasy" which stems from a disappointed love for her father.

I have to renounce him – because he has a mistress . . .

As a result, she renounces all men and represses her femininity in favour of an identification with masculinity.

Lesbianism and Feminism

Freud did not regard lesbianism as pathological, arguably, in his view, because it was in fact an identification with masculinity.

Just because it doesn't serve the "natural" aim of reproduction, I don't see it as a perversion.

The notion of homosexuality as a "curable" perversion was further challenged in the 1950s.

But it wasn't until the 1970s that feminism sought to reposition lesbianism from a psychoanalytic perspective, by emphasizing the homoerotic bond between *mother and daughter* in the pre-Oedipal phase.

Lesbianism and Irigaray

Irigaray's reading of Freud on female sexuality has exposed the phallocentrism which renders lesbianism invisible in his texts. Rather than regard lesbianism as specifically female, Freud argued that the female homosexual is a woman with a man's desire for a woman-phallus.

The phallic masquerade serves to veil the **double lack** projected onto the lesbian body by the male theorist. He does not acknowledge the circulation of pleasure between women when it is not mediated by **male** desire.

Irigaray calls for a more adequate treatment of female narcissism, which psychoanalysis undermines by repressing the woman's perspective in the imaging and symbolizing of her sexuality. Irigaray deconstructs phallocentric desire by replacing the single male organ with multiple female sex organs, and in this way addresses a female auto-homo-erotic desire not mediated by phallic intervention.

Queer Theory

Queer theorists became an important critical voice in the 1990s. In their view, Foucault's regulatory notions of sexuality do not only refer to heterosexual culture, but can also encompass gay conservative desires for **normativity**. "Queer" is now seen as a transient term, opposed to any and all forms of sexual "normalizations".

"Queer" does not refer to the grand narrative emancipatory struggles of gay subjects.

Instead, it calls into question all reigning schemes of sexual normativity.

Drawing on feminist and postmodern theory, this reconfiguration of the queer subject challenges the understanding of subjectivity which invokes an essentialist biologically-defined sexuality.

An essentialist construction of a homosexual subject has been claimed for political reasons – for instance, the so-called "gay-gene".

But the assumption of an essential gay "identity" consigns subjectivity to biological reductionism which doesn't allow for non-binary difference.

Queer politics challenges the essentialist assumption that "the queer" emerges from a uniquely gay sexuality. Queer sexuality expresses a desire for **polymorphous** sexual configurations and fantasies which do not stem from a need to regulate, control and organize the sexual subject according to compulsory identification.

Plural Sexual Practices

Judith Butler (b. 1956), Associate Professor at Johns Hopkins University, further developed Irigaray's idea that the female homosexual subject is not representable in phallocentric psychoanalysis.

Like Foucault, she argues that "the law of incest" is a mythic construct which structuralist theories of anthropology and psychoanalysis use to understand and naturalize patriarchy.

Butler also agrees with Foucault's idea that the "law" is **generative** rather than repressive.

It therefore produces a binary discourse of transgressive homosexuality versus normative heterosexuality.

Butler rejects the idea of a pre-Oedipal female homosexuality. Rather than celebrating the notion of a female imaginary, or attempting to reconceptualize the imaginary-symbolic order, she argues that because the law is not in fact conceived as rigid, it can be decentred by calling for a plurality of sexual practices.

Performative Identification

Butler's argument is that "naturalized identity" produces the effect of being the norm through the repetition of its performance. But she distinguishes two types of repetition. Repetition can *either* serve the interests of conservative culture by emphasizing its **foundational narratives**; *or* it can resist dominant cultural signification by emphasizing and therefore revealing its **fictions**.

"Performative identification" can either be employed to establish heterosexuality as compulsory – or to reveal its fictitious nature.

Butler is indebted to Fredric Jameson's idea of pastiche as a postmodern form of parody. For her, it is more effective to think of lesbianism as a parody of heterosexuality, rather than "other" to the norms of heterosexuality.

Butler also adopts Joan Riviere's idea of feminine "masquerade" which can preserve or subvert the norms of masculinity. Lesbianism acts in the same way – either to parody the norms of heterosexual culture or to subvert them.

Allo- and Auto-Identification

Eve Kosofsky Sedgwick in **Epistemology of the Closet** (1990), develops Foucault's claim that homosexuality first came to be institutionally recognized and therefore pathologized as a perversion in 1870. "People are different from each other. And we are not always the same as ourselves."

Because people are different, "allo-identification" (identification with the other) should take place. But this rarely does. Allo-identification can make people recognize that they are different from each other. But the subject needs to recognize that "auto-identity" does not take place once and for all.

For Sedgwick, lesbian and gay theory implies both auto- and allo-identification in order to remain different, but not other to each other. She also distinguishes between the categories of gender and sexuality, which are not necessarily interdependent.

Deconstructing Derrida

Gayatri Chakravorty Spivak (b. 1941), Professor of Literature at the University of Pittsburgh, questions the process of deconstruction in relation to gender. For her, Derrida has employed the category of woman to reaffirm the discourse of man. But she also thinks that deconstruction can be employed as a feminist strategy. Although Derrida has criticized phallocentric discourses, Spivak argues that he appropriates the "displacement of woman". She explains this "displacement" by the example of the orgasm which women can simulate but men cannot.

If man signifies presence, woman *displaces* presence. Deconstruction tries to analyze this uncertainty of presence in textuality and the operation of writing.

Deconstructing the Hymen

Spivak puts into question the process of deconstruction in relation to gender. For instance, Derrida refers to the *hymen* as a "feminine veil" – a "mimetic" textual strategy which is constantly retreating behind a series of folds. For Derrida, the masquerading hymen destabilizes the **symbolic presence** signified by the phallus.

Like the female orgasm, the hymen can be both itself and not itself.

It can be metaphorically broken or remain intact.

It exists both within and outside the body.

The hymen signifies both virginity and marriage. Virginity is situated within the law of the phallus, which is also the law of **textual operation**.

The Questioning ~~Woman~~

However, if the phallus is taken as the figure of the law in textual operation, the hymen as a masquerading "thing" becomes doubly displaced within a phallocentric model, because the phallus is **symbolic** and the penis is not.

In this context of displacement and uncertainty, a language of women's desire is made impossible.

For deconstruction to become available to feminist practice, the category of "woman" must not be taken as an object of analysis. Rather, Spivak proposes that the feminist deconstructivist must ask: "What is man that the itinerary of his desire creates such a text?" In this way, woman can be restored to the position of the questioning subject.

Postcolonial or Subaltern Muteness

Spivak also confronts the "muteness" of woman in postcolonial society. She combines feminist and poststructuralist techniques with postcolonial studies to draw attention to the colonial subject, the "doubly oppressed native woman". For Spivak, does the native collude in the formation of otherness and voicelessness? Spivak has argued that under British imperialism the "native", in particular the "native female", was rendered mute.

The subaltern cannot speak.

I first used "subaltern" to describe exploited marginal groups who lack class-consciousness.

Antonio Gramsci (1891–1937), Italian Marxist militant and theorist, employed the term "subaltern" in 1934. He developed a **theory of hegemony** to explain why an exploited or subaltern class accepts domination, when according to Marxist theory it should oppose it. For Gramsci, comparably to Foucault, domination does not simply depend on "state repression" but on persuading the whole of society that the prevailing *thinking* of the ruling class is the only natural and normal one, thereby gaining its hegemony.

Spivak is a member of the **Subaltern Studies Collective**, based at Delhi University, which investigates Indian colonial history. Its aim is to establish a subaltern or peasant consciousness independent of any hegemonic élite. In this perspective, Spivak questions the essentialist assumption of a subject who speaks from a position of knowledge in terms of *identity* (race, gender, class, etc.) rather than *difference*.

"Can men theorize feminism, can whites theorize racism, can the bourgeois theorize revolution, and so on. It is *only* when the former groups theorize that the situation is politically intolerable. Therefore it is crucial that members of these groups are kept vigilant about their assigned subject positions . . . (The position that only the subaltern can know the subaltern, only women can know women and so on, cannot be held as a theoretical presupposition either, for it predicates the possibility of knowledge on identity. Whatever the political necessity for holding the position, and whatever the advisability of attempting to 'identify' (with) the other as subject in order to know her, knowledge is made possible and sustained by irreducible difference, not identity.)"

Who Speaks in Multiculturalism?

All efforts to encompass a "situated subject" can only fail to be complete. All attempts to speak "on behalf of" a putative group can only produce conceptual mismatches.

Once a society becomes multicultural, central institutions begin to choose representatives from various cultural groups to "speak as" a spokesperson for a set of people. Spivak questions the authenticity that this process of selection entails.

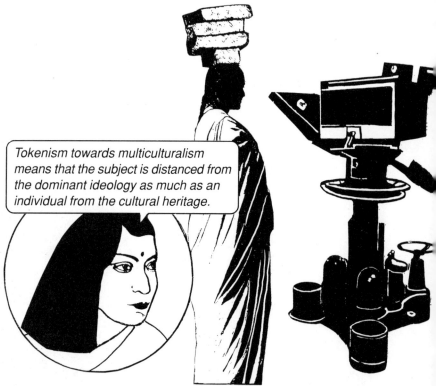

Tokenism towards multiculturalism means that the subject is distanced from the dominant ideology as much as an individual from the cultural heritage.

However, Spivak sees the positive effects of this "inauthenticity", because it highlights the decline of monoculturalism and the history that gave rise to contemporary multiculturalism.

Postfeminism and postcolonial studies have converged to question the totalizing or colonizing tendencies of Western feminist scholarship. Proper critical attention is thereby paid to colonial subjects *doubly colonized* by imperial as well as patriarchal ideologies.

Race and Psychoanalysis

Frantz Fanon (1925–61), born on the French Caribbean island of Martinique, studied medicine and psychiatry in France. He worked as a psychoanalyst in a hospital in Algeria during the mid-1950s, at the crucial beginning of Algeria's struggle to liberate itself from French colonial rule. Fanon strongly identified with Algerian national independence. He was one of the first to address the issues of imperialism and race in terms of a liberationist psychoanalysis. Fanon theorized the position of the racially oppressed in relation to the Oedipus Complex. The oppressed subject could be understood as the angry son who wishes to kill the father – the white man.

According to Fanon's theory, the violence inscribed in the idea of "self" (or victim) and "other" (or oppressor) presumes a unified human subject. The subject is understood as having a free will outside the order of language. Feminists have questioned the notion that the "other" can only be conceived within a framework of violence.

Race, Feminism and Psychoanalysis

Psychoanalytic theory has not been deployed by black feminist critical theorists. This is because of the "Oedipal paradigm". Freud, in **Totem and Taboo** (1912–13), claimed that all culture is rooted in the Oedipus Complex. This elides all the specificity of cultural differences by positing a single *universal* psyche. Psychoanalysis thus becomes equivalent to colonialization.

To enter the symbolic order, the subject must submit to phallocentrism and colonialization.

Culture and cultural authority are not only given as **masculine**, but as **transhistorical**.

This does not allow for social intervention or historical agency. Black women not only have to negotiate their identity in terms of a phallogocentric symbolic order, but also within the colonialist subordination of black identity.

Woman in psychoanalysis has been metaphorically located as the "dark continent", Africa. Feminism has therefore been correct to interpret woman as a colonized subject.

White feminism has theorized the colonialization of **all** women who are subjected to patriarchal oppression.

But black feminists have found this positioning problematic. It ignores specific cultural conditions in favour of a "global sisterhood".

Postmodernism and Black Experience

bell hooks (b. 1955) questions the relevance of postmodernism to African American politics.

While postmodern discourses draw attention to the experience of otherness and difference, they are at the same time understood by African Americans as exclusionary because they lack concrete relevance to real conditions of marginality.

Because postmodernism is identified with a reaction to the specific Western phenomenon of "high modernism", there is little reference to the experiences and writing of black people, especially black women.

"It is sadly ironic that the contemporary discourse which talks the most about heterogeneity, the decentered subject, declaring breakthroughs that allow recognition of Otherness, still directs its critical voice primarily to a specialized audience that shares a common language rooted in the master narratives it claims to challenge."

hooks also criticizes postmodern "anti-essentialist discourses" in relation to black identities which she argues are still struggling for recognition.

But I am also critical of notions of "black authenticity" which homogenize difference.

Whatever the validity of postmodern discourses in relation to black identity, she is concerned that these must not remain exclusively located in the predominantly white institution of the university.

Orientalism

Edward Said (b. 1935), Professor of English and Comparative Literature at Columbia University, established **Orientalism** as a set of representations which have constructed a Western prejudicial view of the Orient – everything that is not understood as European.

*"The Orient" does not exist as a natural category. It is produced within the domain of Orientalism in which the Western subject **knows** and **masters** the Eastern object.*

Orientalism shows how power dynamics between East and West operate according to this system. Said draws on Foucault's concept of discourse as a system of regulation. This process of regulation occurs precisely through the power invested in *knowledge* itself.

Through a range of diverse fields – history, geography, science, culture, travel, exploration and wars of conquest – the West has produced cultural meanings which offer a detailed authoritative knowledge of the Orient.

Although fictional, these versions of the Orient eventually come to be regarded as "natural", so that the original political motivations which produced them are no longer evident.

The discourse of Orientalism is therefore one of power and domination. But it also establishes a Lacanian "dialectic of difference". The West constructs its own fictional "self-identity" by producing the Orient as its Other – what Said calls "its deepest and most recurring (image) of the Other". The category of the "White Man" (Said always refers to the subject as man) is like that of the "Oriental", a fictional construct which is produced as natural, and whose political effects remain disguised.

Feminism and Moral Philosophy

Until recently, women were deliberately excluded from professional philosophy. Feminist philosophers have argued that Western philosophy is a key component of a masculine culture of confrontation that can never be "objective" or "neutral". They are deeply sceptical of traditional male forms of ethical philosophy.

Although today women are becoming increasingly involved in moral philosophy, they do not necessarily consider themselves feminist. Some prefer to be perceived as "women philosophers".

Feminism has questioned the assumption that ethics can be gender neutral.

Postfeminism acknowledges that all discourses are subject positioned.

In order to understand gender positioning in relation to moral philosophy, we need to deconstruct the role of gender in traditional ethical philosophy.

Traditional Ethical Philosophy

Traditional "liberal" ethical philosophy is founded on the individual who freely chooses to live according to a universal set of principles derived from the objective exercise of "reason". There are various prescriptive definitions of "reason"; but they *all* maintain that the exercise of reason is gender-neutral – the product of a transcendent consciousness, free of any social environment. ***Mary Wollstonecraft*** (1759–97), a founder of liberal feminism in the Enlightenment, agreed with this model of ethics.

> Gender is irrelevant to ethical judgements. **Mind has no sex.**

> To be moral in this sense means believing that you must be **masculinized** to be morally competent.

Feminists have long since understood that ethical philosophy is grounded in a patriarchal definition of "reason" as an exclusively masculine experience. Postfeminism, like postmodernism, has put into question a moral system which relies on a discourse of reason and rationality.

Brief Introduction to Virtue Theory

So, the dilemma is this: if "transcendent reason" and "ethical objectivity" are both fictions; and if the liberal tradition of ethics ignores gender – then what is the basis for a morality which can include the differences between men and women in non-essentialist terms?

The bankruptcy of moral systems means that many modern women philosophers have come to agree with **Aristotle** (384–322 BC) and suggest "virtue theory" as an alternative kind of moral philosophy. These views began to be voiced tentatively in the late 1950s by philosophers like Foot and Anscombe, more loudly and assertively later on by others.

Virtue theory insists that it is misguided to expect reason to be able to establish some infallible moral doctrine which is compulsory and often counter to human nature and emotions. Perhaps morality is not about conforming to rules, but more about being trained to see problematic situations in a moral way. Morality may not be the rational control of the emotions but, more appropriately, the cultivation of desirable emotions. Virtue theorists suggest that philosophers should concentrate more on establishing what makes for good people and good societies. This usually means that morality has to be built on human nature and that acting morally means the realization of one's nature rather than insisting on its denial. Morality has to rest on our beliefs about human beings' fundamental needs and interests, whatever they may be. The job of philosophers is to try to establish what social structures and institutions encourage the fulfilment of human moral potential. Virtue theory inevitably often tends towards a form of "ethical naturalism". Ethical theories tend to be categorized as "naturalist" or "non-naturalist". Non-naturalist theories like those of Plato and Kant depict ethics as something necessarily transcendentally pure and uncontaminated by the world of human desires. Naturalists, like the Utilitarian philosophers, suggest that ethics has to be based on some fundamental truths about human nature, and so can be regarded as true or false. Ethical naturalists believe that morality must be removed from the transcendent and objective and pushed towards being something more human and contingent – so that it becomes something closer to psychology or sociology, or even biology (which raises problems, as we'll see).

What "women's nature" is, is therefore crucial for any feminist ethic. The work of **Carol Gilligan** is seminal in this respect. She claims (**In A Different Voice**, 1982) that women consider moral issues in a different way from men – more as a matter of relationships and intimacy, rather than as one of rights and duties, laws and doctrines. But virtue theory and Ethical Naturalism are themselves highly problematic.

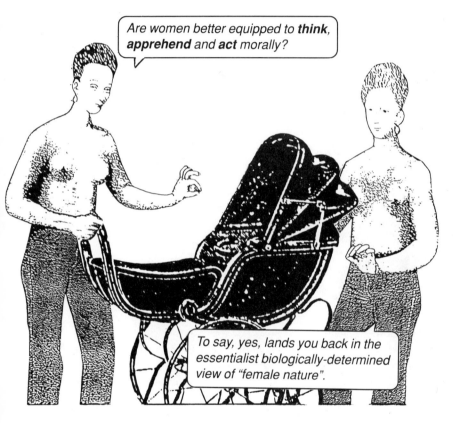

If women are "innately supportive, non-competitive nurturers", they can be all too easily disregarded and feminist ethics marginalized.

Some older established philosophers like Anscombe, Midgley, Foot, and the younger Nussbaum are sympathetic to aspects of virtue theory. Thomson, and among the younger, Haack, are less so; and O'Neill seeks a compromise. Others, like Murdoch (a resolute non-naturalist), Beauvoir and Arendt have an Existentialist agenda.

The Existentialists

Hannah Arendt (1906–75), born in Kant's city of Königsberg, came from a wealthy German-Jewish family. She went to the University of Marburg where she met and subsequently had an affair with the "Existentialist" Martin Heidegger. She was also taught by the phenomenologist Edmund Husserl and the Existentialist Karl Jaspers. She was arrested by the Gestapo in 1933 and had to flee Germany. She lived as a stateless person until 1951 when she became a US citizen. In **The Human Condition** (1958) she agrees with Heidegger.

Ethical philosophy has to begin with the fact that human beings are active participants in the world who make choices.

*But I disagree with your essentialist insensitivity to human **differences** – those of racial identities and gender.*

Much of Arendt's philosophical work applies phenomenological and Existentialist methods to political issues – especially the causes and effects of 20th century Totalitarianism. She is probably most famous for her book **Eichmann in Jerusalem: A Report on the Banality of Evil** (1964). This addresses the moral emptiness of bureaucratic administrators like Adolf Eichmann who organized the industrial scale of the Holocaust – a new kind of 20th century evil. Towards the end of her life, she took up the problem of moral responsibility in her book **The Life of the Mind** (1978), an analysis of thinking, willing and judging.

We have already seen (page 10) that **Simone de Beauvoir** was a key figure of socialist feminism in the FR movement. Her philosophy employed the insights of an Existentialism developed in the 1940s by her companion **Jean-Paul Sartre** (1905–80). Sartrean Existentialism insists that the individual can only achieve *authentic being* by choosing to be free, whatever the cost.

*Women are socialized into becoming **inauthentic** beings with no real personal autonomy.*

The view of "female nature" – irrational, selfless and passive – is really an ideological construct to legitimize male supremacy.

Existentialism in the 1950s rescued moral philosophy from the impasse of **logical positivism** which argued that only disputes about *facts* could be resolved; moral disputes could not. Issues of morals or politics were merely "emotional evaluations" and therefore, in purely logical terms, *non*-sense. To reject emotion as non-philosophical could also serve to categorize woman as irrational and therefore disqualified from philosophy.

Beauvoir, like Sartre and other Existentialists, used fiction-writing to illustrate the human issues of choice and self-deception. *Iris Murdoch* (b. 1919) is another moral philosopher renowned for a similar practice. Her novels are richly comic but serious. Murdoch's first published work was on Sartre. She studied at Somerville College, Oxford, and became a fellow of St Anne's College, Oxford.

As an ethical philosopher, Murdoch began as an Existentialist, but later became an eccentric Christian Platonist. In **Metaphysics as a Guide to Morals** (1993), she explains her belief in a transcendent Good.

Beauty is the visible and accessible aspect of the Good. But because the Good is not itself visible, knowledge of it has to be reached through a study and understanding of great works of art.

In her later work, **Existentialists and Mystics** (1997), Murdoch reiterates how art is useful in enabling you to perceive and evaluate moral situations more disinterestedly.

Virtue Theorists

Phillipa Foot (b. 1920) is Professor of Philosophy at the University of California. She was one the first moral philosophers to reintroduce the relevance and authority of "virtue theory", which maintains that the central question for ethical philosophy is not what the rules are, but what a moral person is actually like. Foot is probably most famous for two articles written in 1958 (**Moral Arguments**, **Moral Beliefs**).

Moral beliefs concern dispositions to behave in certain ways that can subsequently be labelled as moral, but cannot be arrived at through some form of "moral reasoning".

For her, "moral objectivity" and "a transcendent viewpoint" are both fictions. Moral considerations "are necessarily related in some way to good and harm". In **Virtues and Vices** (1978) she maintains her relativist and naturalist position that what counts as "virtuous" may change.

Elizabeth Anscombe (b. 1919) was a pupil of Wittgenstein, and one of his literary executors. She produced an important introduction to Wittgenstein's **Tractatus**. She is a member of the British analytical school of philosophy and has written extensively on logic and language. Her first book, **Intentions** (1957), examines the role of intentional expressions and actions in ethical concepts and behaviour. Perhaps her most famous paper is **Modern Moral Philosophy** (1958), in which she argued that traditional moral doctrines no longer make much sense in the modern world because they ignore human needs and desires. Her account of morality is clearly influenced by Wittgenstein's philosophy of language.

Morality is a kind of language game and cannot "transcend" the community from which it originates.

Morality is created out of social conditions. Ethical principles may simply be practices and behaviour which enable social groups to flourish in history.

Anscombe is another advocate of virtue theory. Any account of morality has to take note of how and why people feel an emotional commitment to those around them. It is important to examine motives and desires, as well as principles, and ask to what extent we are responsible for our own moral character. Anscombe is very aware of how this kind of "sociological" explanation of morality can lead to the usual problems of relativism and determinism.

Judith Jarvis Thomson (b. 1929) is an American philosopher who believes that moral **rights** are central to any philosophical account of morality. She is undoubtedly most famous for her essay **A Defense of Abortion** (1971), in which she defends the permissibility of abortion with a persuasive but much-disputed analogy. She maintains that a pregnant woman and her unborn child are similar to a blood-donor "attached" to a kidney patient with a rare blood group who requires her charitable assistance to survive.

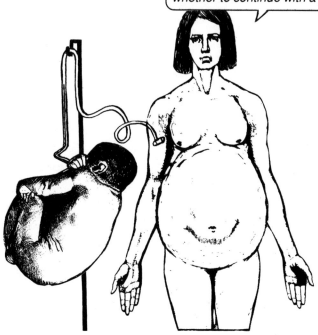

Just as we feel only the donor has the right to decide whether or not to continue to supply her blood – so a mother ultimately has the right to decide whether to continue with a pregnancy.

There is no other case in law in which a woman must sacrifice her own self-determination and bodily integrity in order to preserve the lives of others. Professor Thomson is also the author of **The Realm of Rights** (1990) in which she explores issues like the permanence and negotiability of moral rights.

Mary Warnock (b. 1924) has been Headmistress of Oxford High School as well as Mistress of Girton College, Cambridge. Her early works were on Existentialist ethics but she later centred on the philosophy of mind (**Imagination**, 1976 and **Memory**, 1987). She chaired the Committee of Inquiry into Human Fertilization and in 1985 became well-known for **The Warnock Report on Human Fertilization and Embryology**. She contributes to public debates on education and is frequently asked to pronounce on practical ethical issues in the media. In 1996, she wrote introductions to the Dent series on *Women Philosophers*.

Education is an ethical concern . . .

Any conflict between Kantian ethics and virtue theory is usually a false one.

Onora O'Neill (b. 1941), Principal of Newnham College, Cambridge, is an expert on Kantian ethics. She has written widely on poverty, justice and development, and on topics of equal opportunities, children's rights and environmental ethics. In **Towards Justice and Virtue** (1998) she attempts to reconcile Kantian ethical philosophy with virtue theory.

Mary Midgley (b. 1919) is a professional philosopher with considerable knowledge of biology that she uses to examine environmental and gender issues. She spells out very clearly the philosophical problems facing feminism in **Women's Choices** (1983). Midgley is another ethical naturalist and virtue theorist. She is deeply critical of crude Darwinian or socio-biological and genetic explanations of human behaviour.

Given our natures, there are certain kinds of lives human beings will find fulfilling. Human morality is rooted in biology but not reducible to it.

Ethical beliefs need to be binding, rational and morally credible (**Beast and Man**, 1978). In **The Ethical Primate** (1994), she explores how our evolutionary origins may influence the extent and limitations of human freedom. She continually stresses the limitations of science and what it can achieve (**Science and Salvation**, 1992). Midgley is nowadays best known for her writings on the moral status of animals and the environment (**Animals and Why they Matter**, 1984).

Susan Haack (b. 1945) was Professor of Philosophy at the University of Warwick and now teaches in the USA at various universities. She is a philosopher of logic and science, best known for her work on the philosophical implications of "fuzzy logic". Fuzzy logic is important in some areas of computer science and artificial intelligence.

In **Deviant Logic** (1974), Haack stresses that there can be a logic of fuzziness, but not a fuzzy logic. She has also written on the philosophy of pragmatism and its relevance to philosophical explanations of scientific method and theory. She is highly critical of the epistemological relativism of some postmodernist philosophers like Richard Rorty. She has written on gender issues, notably in **Science from a Feminist Perspective** (1992). In **Manifesto of a Passionate Moderate** (1998) she is critical of some feminist philosophical assertions about the cultural or gender relativism of philosophy and scientific inquiry.

Martha Nussbaum (b. 1947) is best-known for her work on Greek and Roman philosophy. In **The Fragility of Goodness** (1986) she explored the overlap areas where Greek philosophers and playwrights consider the role of luck in ethical decision-making. **Love's Knowledge** (1992) examines literature as another form of ethical inquiry. Literature is essential because it is a way of testing moral theory to see if it "works". Nussbaum stresses the importance of emotions in ethical evaluation and decision-making.

In her most recent book, **Cultivating Humanity** (1997), she cites ancient philosophers like Socrates and Seneca in order to defend multiculturalist studies in American universities.

A true community of scholars should be made up of self-critical world citizens, encouraged to transcend the boundaries of class, gender and nationality.

Nussbaum defends gender studies against charges of moral relativism and low standards. She has edited a book on **Women, Culture and Development** (1996) which probes the mostly disastrous political, economic and moral relations that exist between developing countries and the affluent Western nations.

Genetic Engineering and Ethics

Feminist moral philosophers have played a key role in improving legislation in favour of women's rights, e.g., abortion. And, as we have seen, they have been active in questioning today's most crucially important ethical issues: biological determination, gender difference, children's rights, environmental ethics, scientific ethics and embryology.

Does a post-menopausal woman have the right to bear a child?

In the future, the demands on moral philosophy to unpack ethical dilemmas will increase as genetic engineering intrudes into our everyday lives. For example, procreation will not hold the same biological constraints for women. The ethics of fertilization and human cloning have already become ideological and moral minefields.

Cyberfeminism

Cyberfeminism positively affirms and celebrates the postmodern digital information revolution, artificial intelligence and telematics. This is postfeminism in its technological manifestation. It is useful to remind ourselves of the origins of "cyber" and other related terms.

The prefix *cyber* derives from *cybernetics* (from the Greek, *kybernetes*, meaning helmsman) coined by a professor of mathematics, Norbert Wiener, in 1947. Cybernetics is a general theory of self-regulating and control systems. It is a science of systems of control and communications in animals and machines.

From this systems theory we get *cyberspace*: a term coined by the science fiction writer William Gibson to define the computer-generated multisensory experience of virtual reality and the globally interactive space on the Internet.

Cyborg is a human subject augmented by chemicals, bionic prosthesis and neural implants. The cyborg differs from the earlier mechanical automaton, the robot (from the Czech, *robota*, forced labour, first used in K.Čapek's play, *R.U.R.*), and also from the android, a robot in apparently human form.

Donna Haraway (b. 1944), Professor in the History of Consciousness Board at the University of California, Santa Cruz, issued **A Cyborg Manifesto** in 1991. This is an analysis of feminism in the advanced technological conditions of postmodern life in the Western world. Haraway employs Marxist, psychoanalytic and feminist methodologies to analyze how discourses of race, gender and class have been transformed by technological developments.

But I problematize each of these older humanist methodologies . . .

We shall now see how she deals with these established discourses . . .

Versus Marxism, Psychoanalysis and . . .

Marxist humanism understands the subject in terms of a labour theory of value and a Western sense of self.

Psychoanalysis relies on the family and the birth of the self – which in the Lacanian imaginary asserts wholeness before language.

*Marxism does not acknowledge **cultural difference** as articulated in anti-colonial discourse and practice.*

Both Freudian and Lacanian psychoanalysis construct the category of women as other. In this context, women are either idealized or undermined.

But in both contexts, women are presumed inferior, having a weaker sense of self, weaker individuation, a stronger association to the Mother and to the **oral** rather than the **written** (the preferred "technology" of the cyborg, as it is for Derrida).

. . . feminism

What about **feminism**? There is nothing about being female that naturally binds women. There is not even such a state as "being" female, itself a highly complex category constructed by scientific discourses and other social practices that are now challenged.

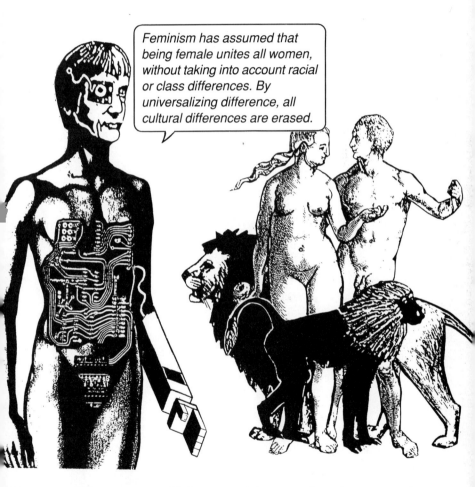

Feminism has assumed that being female unites all women, without taking into account racial or class differences. By universalizing difference, all cultural differences are erased.

Haraway rejects woman as childbearer and the compulsory heterosexual nuclear family. She opposes the concept of individual wholeness and completeness, Biblical hierarchies (god/man/animal), fear of death and automatism. She challenges the Freudian family drama and the Lacanian m/other and attempts to destabilize binary oppositions which she believes have conspired to oppress minorities.

The Cyborg Self

Haraway deploys the **cyborg** as the relevant postmodern metaphor for woman. **Technology** is radically restructuring the world. "Cultural discourse" itself and women (due to lack of education and training) are not participating and learning to control these technologies.

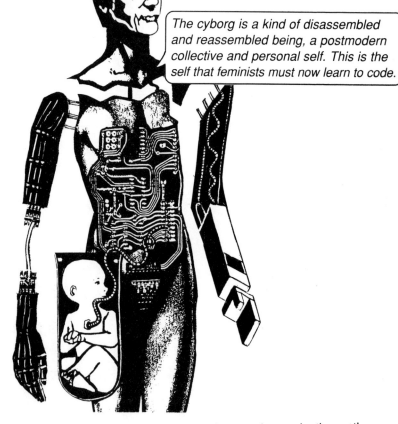

The cyborg is a kind of disassembled and reassembled being, a postmodern collective and personal self. This is the self that feminists must now learn to code.

Cyborg replication does not rely on organic sexual reproduction or the organic nuclear family. The cyborg is both animal and machine; both fiction and social reality. The cyborg breaks down the traditional humanist barriers: human versus animal, human versus machine and physical versus non-physical. The cyborg is the "illegitimate child of patriarchy, colonialism and capitalism".

Postfeminism as Cyber-virus

Sadie Plant (b. 1964), another techno-theorist, claims that machines in patriarchal culture are female because they are unpredictable and men work on them. They lack agency, autonomy and self-awareness. Men use technology as a way of developing their supremacy. Plant quotes Irigaray: "There is only one species, and it is male: homo sapiens. There are no other sapiens. Woman is virtual reality."

The text is patriarchal – but **hypertext** which is non-linear disrupts patriarchal narratives.

Hypertext is electronic text that allows the reader to move non-sequentially through information. It is now the key technology of the World Wide Web. Plant argues that digitalization is similar to the traditionally female art of weaving. In her view, technology has now become "vulnerable to cyberfeminist infection".

Feminist Cyberpunk

"Cyberpunk" is a term first used by critics to describe William Gibson's influential sci-fi novel *Neuromancer* (1984). Cyberpunk is an eclectic hotch-potch, but in essence it welcomes the intrusion of technology into human lives. A paranoid dystopian future becomes the present. There is no scope for progress or humanism. Global corporations rather than governments hold power. Hackers are anarchic revolutionaries.

Cyberpunk feminist writers, such as **Kathy Acker** (1947–97), are celebrating a virtual world where disembodied subjects see gender-positioning as optional.

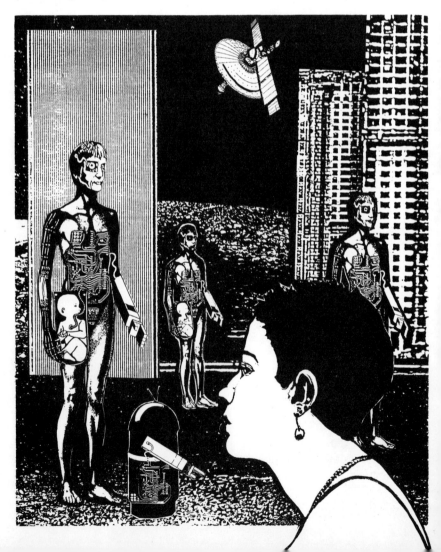

Postfeminism and Film Theory

In the late 1960s and early 1970s, film theorists began employing psychoanalysis to explain how films and the cinema work at an unconscious level. Christian Metz and other structuralists drew on Freud's theory of instinctual libido drives and Lacan's mirror phase. This combination offered a model of cinematic representation which "constructs" the spectator through the re-enactment of unconscious processes involved in the acquisition of language and sexual difference.

The three main concerns of psychoanalytic film theory were . . .

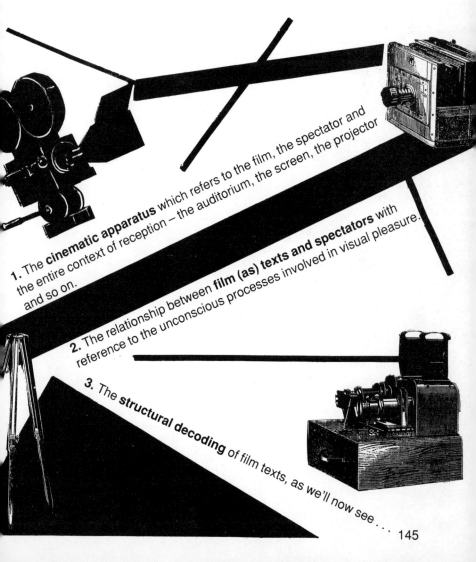

1. The **cinematic apparatus** which refers to the film, the spectator and the entire context of reception – the auditorium, the screen, the projector and so on.

2. The relationship between **film (as) texts and spectators** with reference to the unconscious processes involved in visual pleasure.

3. The **structural decoding** of film texts, as we'll now see . . .

Laura Mulvey (b. 1941), feminist film theorist and film-maker, wrote the seminal essay **Visual Pleasure in Narrative Cinema** (1975).

The cinema is determined by the patriarchal unconscious which produces and reproduces the male gaze. This gaze is voyeuristic and fetishistic.

Mulvey sought to analyze and destroy the pleasure in watching the classic Hollywood films which encourage women to see themselves as objects of desire – and which in turn forces women to see themselves narcissistically.

For Mulvey, the visual gaze is framed in binaries: narcissism/desire, looking/being looked at, active/passive, masculine/feminine.

In Hollywood cinema, men are invited to identify with the male protagonist in desiring the woman as object.

Women identify with the passivity of the female subjects and therefore any active desire becomes erased.

The male viewer masters the woman's otherness either through sadistic voyeurism or fetishism.

The Cinematic Gaze

Let's consider the terms Mulvey identifies as implicated in the "cinematic gaze".

Voyeurism: a term used by Freud to analyze the erotic gratification of a peeping Tom who watches without being seen in order to alleviate a castration anxiety.

Scopophilia or Scopic Drive: pleasurable looking, a drive instinct. This concept was developed by Freud from its origin in the infantile libido. The term has been used in psychoanalytic film theory to understand the unconscious processes that are brought into play when the spectator looks at the image on screen.

Fetishism: a term which Freud redesigned to analyze a sexual deviation associated with the fear of castration. In the analytic sense, fetishism is a male response towards women who are seen to lack the phallus. The fetish is a fantasy object erected in place of the lack which is disavowed.

Spectator: a mode of analysis in psychoanalytic film theory which refers to the various "subject positions" constructed by a film. **Audience**, instead, refers to the people in the cinema and is associated with cultural studies.

Mulvey's ideas were further developed by herself and other film theorists. Their aim was twofold: either to seek and emphasize moments of disruptive and transgressive femininity; or to theorize the cinematic representation as the *mise-en-scène* (staging) of desire and the site of fantasy, which thereby offers multiple subject positions, both male and female.

Jacqueline Rose (b. 1949) is Lecturer in the School of English and Drama at Queen Mary and Westfield College, University of London. In **Sexuality in the Field of Vision** (1986), Rose examines the political significance of vision in the paradigms put forward by Freudian and Lacanian psychoanalysis to explain the realization of sexual difference and the castration complex. The female subject in art, film and literature is represented as deficient or lacking.

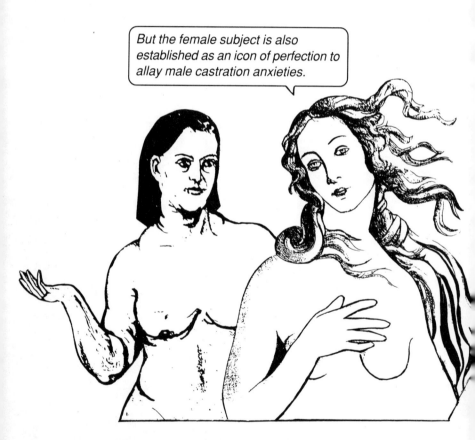

But the female subject is also established as an icon of perfection to allay male castration anxieties.

Women's genitals are often represented without specificity and the female form without a blemish. Freud believes this "absence" represents the female subject as "lacking" in relation to the male. Idealization functions both on the level of content as well as in terms of form.

Postfeminism and Dance

The body is the dance's medium of expression. How we *use* the body – its "messages" coded in social and cultural terms – always has gender implications. Feminists in the 1980s began to explore the disciplined *etiquette* choreographed by patriarchal culture. All forms of dance, from the waltz to ballet, were shaped by the publicly acceptable distance between male and female bodies. Modern dance broke radically from this and contributed to the emancipated expression of woman's body. **Isadora Duncan** (1878–1927) pioneered revolutionary dance techniques that shed the "corset" of rigidly conservative ballet norms – followed by **Martha Graham**.

Dance was marginalized from theory until the work of sociologist of art **Janet Wolff**. Two notable postmodern analysts of dance are **Christy Adair** and **Sally Barnes**. Adair has developed Laura Mulvey's concept of the "male gaze" in cinema practice.

Psychoanalysis and Art Criticism

Freud provided the classic model of psychoanalytic art criticism in a 1910 essay, **Leonardo da Vinci and a Memory of his Childhood**. *Leonardo* (1452–1519) was the illegitimate son of a successful Florentine notary and a country girl who married a peasant when the child was five. He then went to live with his father and young childless wife who became his devoted stepmother. Freud based his psycho-biography on Leonardo's single recorded childhood memory: that when he was in his cradle, a mysterious "vulture" swooped down to open his mouth with its tail – an ambiguous symbol of the breast and the penis.

This fantasy is the key to understanding Leonardo's inability to **complete** his works of art and science.

His father's early abandonment and a fear of surpassing him led to Leonardo's **inhibition**, often reflected in his many unfinished paintings. Paternal authority and a fantasy of the maternal phallus – the vulture's tail, his mother's seduction and the double motherhood – also determined his homosexual object-choice. He avoided all contact with the female body and developed a cult of the masculine body.

Freud denied that psychoanalysis could ever determine the sources of creativity.

My aim is to reconstruct Leonardo's destiny from the starting-point of an illusion.

Some of Freud's colleagues "discovered" the outline of a vulture in Leonardo's painting of St Anne – and thus attempted to put the fantasy into the realm of reality.

The Maternal in Art

Kristeva takes a different approach to Freud in her 1980 study of the Renaissance painter *Giovanni Bellini* (1430?–1516). She works from the paintings rather than the scarce biographical details. Her interest is in the significance of the maternal body revealed in Bellini's art.

This is the painter of motherhood above all.

Kristeva sees Bellini's maternal figures absorbed by the "baby-object of all desire, ineffable *jouissance*", while instead Leonardo's maternal figures are absent. Although there is nothing "feminist" in Bellini's painterly action, yet he provides motherhood with a language that reaches the threshold of **maternal** *jouissance*.

Psychoanalysis and the Maternal

For Freud, the memory of the pre-phallic mother is remote and difficult to access in psychoanalysis.

Everything in this first attachment to the mother seemed to me so difficult to grasp in analysis – so grey with age and shadowy and almost impossible to revivify – that it was as if it had succumbed to an especially inexorable repression.

Lacan's re-reading of the maternal obscures her figure even further, as we'll now see.

Lacan's Pre-Linguistic Maternal

According to Lacan, the infant child's primary relationship and radical dependency on the maternal body, termed the **Imaginary**, is repressed when the child enters the **Symbolic** order. The Symbolic is the order of paternal law which structures all linguistic signification. The Symbolic can only become possible by the child's rejection of its libidinal drives towards the maternal body. The Symbolic represses the **libidinal multiplicity** and chaos of the Imaginary into a **univocal language** structured by the law.

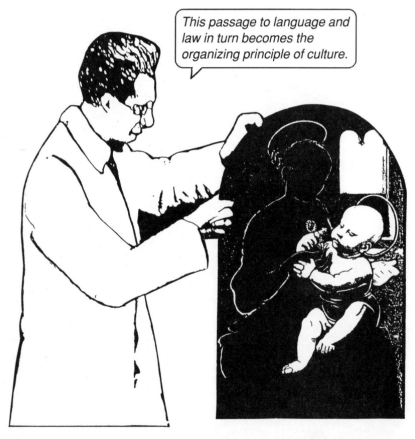

This passage to language and law in turn becomes the organizing principle of culture.

The Imaginary is defined in contra-distinction to the Symbolic and is associated to the pre-Oedipal, pre-linguistic maternal. For Lacan, the Imaginary is conservative and comforting, tending towards closure. It is therefore disrupted by the Symbolic.

Kristeva's Semiotic Maternal

Kristeva reverses Lacan's notion. For her, it is the **semiotic** which is revolutionary, breaks closure and disrupts the Symbolic. Kristeva's semiotic is the pre-discursive, the pre-verbal, which has to do with rhythm, tone, colour and all that which is **pre-representational**. For Kristeva, the semiotic becomes the "unrepresentable" in art, but is nevertheless *present* in it and in the poetic register of language.

"The semiotic is a more immediate expression of the drives and is linked to the bodily contact to the mother before the paternal order of language comes to separate the subject from the mother. Although the semiotic is found in the sounds of pre-linguistic children, the semiotic is always present and traversing language, a bodily presence disruptive to the sublimated symbolic order."

Kristeva's notion of the pre-Oedipal semiotic is, however, distinct from the mother as *speaking subject* in the Symbolic order.

A Criticism of Kristeva

In **Feminism and Psychoanalysis: The Daughter's Seduction** (1982) **Jane Gallop** argues that the danger with Kristeva's theory is that the semiotic may "fall" into the Imaginary – and therefore the potential disrupting element of the maternal may in fact become a comforting representation, similar to the Lacanian notion of the Imaginary.

"This difficulty and the incompatibility between the Lacanian Imaginary and the Kristevan semiotic can be taken as the locus of conflict between the two maternals, one conservative, the other dissident as a way of keeping the mother 'both double and foreign' and therefore guarding between a complacent assimilation of the mother on one hand and against a notion of superior dissidence on the other."

Art and the Maternal

The maternal in Western culture is ubiquitously represented in the figure of the Virgin Mary. Christian iconography of the Virgin Mother is without doubt the most sophisticated symbolic construct in which femininity, to the extent that it figures therein – and it does so constantly – is confined within the limits of the maternal.

In the 1970s and 80s, several women artists, informed by feminist psychoanalytic discourses, explored the representation of the maternal.

Mary Kelly's **Post-Partum Document** (1973–78) was initially an installation in which she explored the mother-child relationship. The document, which exists in six parts, is informed by the key stages in the psychoanalytic development of this relationship. It reveals the changes and reactions the relationship goes through over a period of four and a half years. Mary Kelly constructs an archaeology of the female subject which is drawn from an autobiographical case history.

"We have a configuration of objects and texts where the so-called representational images of the woman may be absent but her presence is traced or felt or visualized in a way that will convey the sense, the implication, of her desire in that relationship."

Postfeminist Art Criticism

In the 1970s, feminism challenged the "phallic criticism" of male writings on women artists based on biological clichés of femininity. Feminist artists and writers began to explore the impact of language, privilege and oppression in relation to gender, sexuality, class and race. In the 1980s, postfeminist art and criticism became increasingly located in linguistic, philosophical and psychoanalytic discourses.

Visual representation became a crucial area of analysis for feminist critical practitioners for two reasons.

The image of "woman" can only exist as an icon in a phallocentric regime of sexual difference in which the gaze becomes appropriated as masculine and phallic.

*Femininity remains unrepresented and **unrepresentable** within a patriarchal regime.*

Feminist representations of woman attempted to disrupt these "negative" mainstream forms.

From Avantgarde to Postmodern Art

In the first decades of the 20th century,
the modernist avantgarde arose in
opposition to mainstream traditions.
By its formal experiments, its shocking
innovations and radical politics, the
avantgarde defined itself *against* the
dominant culture. Avantgarde practices
challenged the capitalist system,
kitsch and popular art, and thus created
an élitist dichotomy between "quality" or
political art and entertainment for the masses.

The avantgarde was often identified
with socialist or anarchistic utopian
ideologies, ideals rooted in the
Enlightenment's reliance on emancipation
and progress to create a new world order.

The "heroic" phase of modernism was
concerned with revolutionizing society
by means of formalism, experimentation
and technical innovation. Avantgarde
modernism understood itself as an
expression of authenticity, originality and
authorship – a revelation of the true self.

Two Views of Avantgardism

Rosalind Krauss is Professor of Modern Art and Theory at Columbia University in New York, and editor of the influential *October* magazine. The avant-garde in Krauss's view is a function of the discourse of **originality**. But the actual practice of "vanguard art" reveals that originality is in fact an assumption that stems from repetition and recurrence.

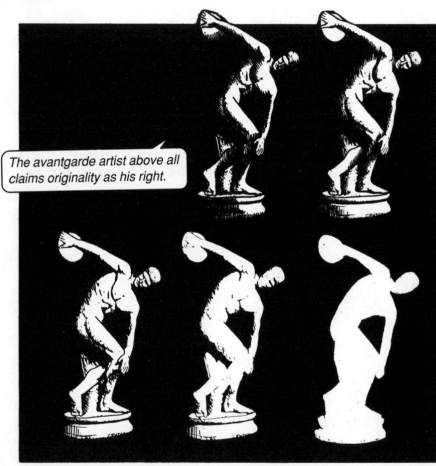

The avantgarde artist above all claims originality as his right.

By deconstructing the notion of *origin* and *originality*, postmodernism seeks to establish an historical divide between itself and the avantgarde, to avoid the avantgarde's basic presuppositions and to expose its fictitious nature. This fictitious nature is the idea that transgression can only take place within the terms of artistic creation *already established*, in other words, in a process of repetition that claims originality.

Kriteva has been critical of Derrida's *différance*. She acknowledges that it unsettles and disturbs logic, but it fails to account for the disruptive force which constitutes change. Because deconstruction refutes the concept of negativity (the privileging of the first term in the binary oppositional structure, e.g., male over female), it cannot allow for the ruptures which according to Kristeva are preconditions for subversion and transformation.

~~Speech~~ **Writing**

~~male~~ female

> *Disrupting of meaning can occur in various signifying systems – for instance, in the norms of poetry and art practices – which become symptomatic of wider socio-economic dynamics.*

Avantgarde art can subvert signification by introducing *jouissance* to the social. In avantgarde art, the semiotic transgresses the symbolic order, producing radical signifying practices which transform the social and signifying order. This desire for social transformation is driven by Kristeva's Marxist view of ideology.

Postmodern Artists

Sophie Calle (b. 1953) is a leading contemporary artist who has influenced a generation of young British artists. Her work acknowledges the ubiquitous pleasures of voyeurism, intrusion and sensationalism exploited in the mass media.

Calle represents her own and other people's lives for public investigation. Her best-known work involves following strangers. In **Suite Venitienne** (1980), she arbitrarily followed a man to Venice using disguises and the complicity of strangers. Calle reverses the male habit of "stalking" the female.

Jean Baudrillard's essay on Calle's work has read it as a postmodern sign of **seduction** (a tactic much favoured by Baudrillard himself).

*Desire is staged in the arbitrary act of following. There are no real people, just performances of seduction – a **simulation of love**.*

In **L'Homme au Carnet** (1993), Calle found an address book and built up a profile of her subject from the descriptions and anecdotes listed in it. The results were published in the French newspaper *Libération*.

Cindy Sherman (b. 1954) was initially (1975) inspired by stereotype representations of women in 1950s films. She masqueraded as iconic female characters drawn from the movies, and took photographs of herself in such roles. These photographs looked uncannily like authentic film stills.

She later drew from historical art portraits in "self"-portrayals that emphasize the sexualized role of the female subject in art. In her most recent images, she no longer uses her body. The body has been replaced by mutilated, grotesque, fragmented bits of body which suggest pornographic magazine centrefolds.

Sherman has revealed how film, traditional paintings and the media represent women as sexualized, vulnerable, weak and mad.

Louise Bourgeois, born 1912 in France, has lived in New York for sixty years. Bourgeois' work finally began to receive due critical acclaim in the late 1980s and early 90s. A new generation of critics and curators recognized in her work the concerns that they themselves had become preoccupied with – identity, sexuality, gender and memory.

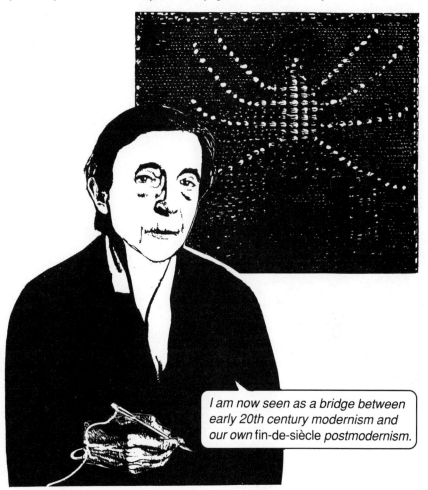

I am now seen as a bridge between early 20th century modernism and our own fin-de-siècle postmodernism.

In the 1960s and 70s her work became explicitly sexual. She is renowned for repeatedly depicting the semi-flaccid penis in sculptures and installations. She draws on personal experience to represent violent emotions such as jealousy, rage and revenge. Her work has been read as a confessional memoir.

Postfeminism into the Future

The 1990s saw a sharp reaction against feminism. Women began to feel alienated by what they saw as the policing of their sexuality. While previous generations had embraced feminist emancipation, younger women claimed to be restricted by what they considered to be prescriptive attitudes on how women should experience their sexual identities. Feminism became reductively identified with political correctness and "victim politics". And yet, paradoxically, these same women are searching for an ideology to express their sexual identities.

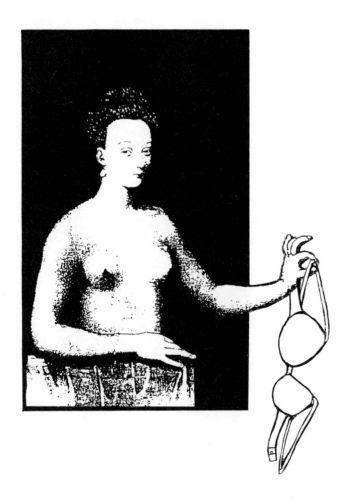

Postfeminism has emerged in response to this need by retaining a desire for empowerment without telling women how to experience their sexuality. By celebrating difference, postfeminism invites women to explore the complexities inscribed in the construction of the sexual subject. Ultimately, feminism and postfeminism will not stand as distinct ideologies, but will be seen to characterize the evolution of a multifaceted discourse which has sought – and will continue to seek – the empowerment of women.

Further Reading

Bookshops and libraries are filled with texts on feminism and postfeminism. Where to begin? The following titles, arranged into main subject areas, are recommended as important and helpful. Some are more advanced and difficult but worth consulting. Readers are advised to start with the *Introducing* series, which includes many relevant titles on feminism, postmodernism, psychoanalysis, cultural studies, sociology and philosophy.

Various authors in this book
These are titles on or by some of the main authors discussed in this book.
Toril Moi (ed.), *The Kristeva Reader* (Blackwell, Oxford and Cambridge, MA 1986)
Juliet Mitchell, *Psychoanalysis and Feminism* (Penguin, London 1974)
André Benjamin (ed.), *The Lyotard Reader* (Blackwell, Oxford and Cambridge, MA 1989)
Paul Rabinow (ed.), *The Foucault Reader: An Introduction to Foucault's Thought* (Penguin, London 1984; Pantheon, New York 1985)
Elizabeth Grosz, *Jacques Lacan, A Feminist Introduction* (Routledge, London and New York 1990)
Peggy Kamuf (ed.), *The Derrida Reader* (Columbia University Press, New York 1991)
Jean Baudrillard, *Simulations*, Semiotext(e) Series (Columbia University Press, New York 1983)
Judith Butler, *Gender Trouble: From Parody to Politics, Feminism and the Subversion of Identity* (Routledge, London and New York 1990)
Alice Jardine, *Gynesis: Configurations of Woman and Modernity* (Cornell University Press, Ithaca, NY 1985)
Camille Paglia, *Sex, Art and American Culture: Essays* (Penguin, London 1993)
Susan Sellers (ed.), *The Hélène Cixous Reader* (Routledge, London and New York 1994)
Margaret Whitford (ed.), *The Irigaray Reader* (Blackwell, Oxford and Cambridge, MA 1991)
Elizabeth Hardwick (ed.), *A Susan Sontag Reader* (Penguin, London 1993)
bell hooks, *Yearning: Race, Gender and Cultural Politics* (South End Press, Cambridge MA 1990)

Feminism and postmodernism
Elaine Marks and Isabelle de Courtivron (eds.), *New French Feminisms* (Harvester, Brighton 1980)
Hal Foster, *Postmodern Culture* (Pluto Press, London and Concord, MA 1985)
Linda J. Nicholson (ed.), *Feminism/Postmodernism* (Routledge, London and New York 1990)
Arthur and Marilouise Kroker (eds.), *Body Invaders: Sexuality and the Postmodern Condition* (Macmillan, Basingstoke 1988)

Feminism and psychoanalysis

J. Laplanche and J.-B. Pontalis, *The Language of Psychoanalysis* (Karnac, London 1973; Norton, New York 1974)

Dylan Evans, *An Introductory Dictionary of Lacanian Psychoanalysis* (Routledge, London and New York 1996)

Elizabeth Wright (ed.), *Feminism and Psychoanalysis: A Critical Dictionary* (Blackwell, Oxford and Cambridge, MA 1992)

Teresa Brennan (ed.), *Between Feminism and Psychoanalysis* (Routledge, London and New York 1989)

Cultural, literary and postcolonial studies

Toril Moi, *Sexual Textual Politics: Feminist Literary Theory* (Routledge, London and New York 1985)

Ann Brooks, *Postfeminism, Feminism, Cultural Theory and Cultural Forms* (Routledge, London and New York 1997)

Anthony Easthope and Kate McGowan (eds.), *A Critical and Cultural Theory Reader* (Open University Press, Milton Keynes 1992)

Simon During (ed.), *The Cultural Studies Reader* (Routledge, London and New York 1993)

Andrew Ross, *No Respect: Intellectuals and Popular Culture* (Routledge, London and New York 1989)

Bill Ashcroft, Gareth Griffiths and Helene Tiffin (eds.), *The Postcolonial Studies Reader* (Routledge, London and New York 1995)

Sexuality, lesbian and gay studies

Lynne Segal and Mary McIntosh (eds.), *Sex Exposed: Sexuality and the Pornography Debate* (Virago, London 1992)

Victor Burgin, James Donald and Cora Kaplan (eds.), *Formations of Fantasy* (Routledge, London and New York 1979)

Lorraine Gamman and Merja Makinen (eds.), *Female Fetishism: A New Look* (Lawrence & Wishart, London 1994)

Henry Abelove, Michele Aina Barate and David M. Halperin (eds.), *The Lesbian and Gay Studies Reader* (Routledge, London and New York 1993)

Film studies

Mandy Merck (ed.), *The Sexual Subject: A Screen Reader in Sexuality* (Routledge, London and New York 1992)

E. Ann Kaplan, *Psychoanalysis and Cinema* (Routledge, London and New York 1990)

Annette Kuhn and Susannah Radstone, *The Woman's Companion to International Film* (Virago, London 1990)

Art studies
Brian Wallis and Marcia Tucker (eds.), *Art After Modernism: Rethinking Representation* (David R. Godine, 1984)
John Berger, *Ways of Seeing* (Penguin, London 1982)

Philosophy and ethics
The literature in these areas is vast. Some key thinkers and their texts have been indicated in this book. Readers who wish to pursue further reading are advised to consult the Philosophy Web Pages on the Internet.
A good one to begin with is **Episteme** (http://www.episteme.com).
See also **Ethics Update Page** (http://ethics.acusd.edu/index.html),
Women in Philosophy(http://billyboy.ius.indiana.edu/Womenin Philosophy/WomeninPhilo-html) and **Feminist Theory Webpage** (http://www.utc.edu/~kswitala/Feminism/Ethics.html).

Dance
Christy Adair, *Women and Dance: Sylphs and Sirens* (Macmillan, Basingstoke 1992)
Sally Barnes, *Dancing Women: Female Bodies on Stage* (Routledge, London and New York 1998)
Janet Wolff, *Aesthetics and the Sociology of Art* (Macmillan, Basingstoke 1993)

Author's Acknowledgements
I would like to thank Ninon Rauh for her assistance. I would like to dedicate the text to Anna Focà.

The author and editor are especially grateful to Dave Robinson for his invaluable contribution to the section on feminist philosophy and ethics. We could not have done it without his help. Our thanks also to Silvia Maroino for her contribution to the page on dance.

Artist's Acknowledgements
Many thanks to Dan Fern, Andrzej Klimowski and Liz Ruth at the Royal College of Art. Thanks also for help and support from Justy, Dominic, Alex, Trang, Ellie, Claudia and the RCA studio. Also Richard Appignanesi for his guidance, and my parents and Al for constant encouragement. Finally, my invaluable models, Sara, Rohan (and Sahosh), Kira, Nerina and especially Leigh, who makes anything possible.

Typesetting by **Wayzgoose**

Sophia Phoca is a critic and lecturer. She is Subject Leader in Time-Based Media at the School of Visual Communication, Kent Institute of Art and Design.

Rebecca Wright graduated from the Royal College of Art and works as an artist in London.

Index